Do It Tomorrow

And Other Secrets of Time Management

D0047676

Also by Mark Forster

Get Everything Done and Still Have Time to Play
How To Make Your Dreams Come True

Do It Tomorrow

And Other Secrets of Time Management

Mark Forster

HODDER &
STOUGHTON

British Library Cataloguing in Publication Data
A record for this book is available from the British Library

ISBN-13: 978 0 340 90912 6

Typeset in Garamond by Avon DataSet Ltd,
Bidford on Avon, Warwickshire

Printed and bound by CPI Group (UK) Ltd, Croydon, CR0 4YY

The paper and board used in this paperback are natural
recyclable products made from wood grown in sustainable
forests. The manufacturing processes conform to the
environmental regulations of the country of origin.

Hodder & Stoughton
A Division of Hodder Headline Ltd
338 Euston Road
London NW1 3BH
www.madaboutbooks.com

To Lucy

Contents

Acknowledgements

I would like to thank my coaching clients and all the people who have attended my seminars on this subject for the immense amount of feedback they have given me, particularly when they've asked the difficult questions.

I also want to acknowledge the support, help and ideas I have had from my wife, Lucy, my coach, Rachel Pryor, and my thinking partners, Katie Rowland and Nadjeschda Hebenstreit.

Quick Start Guide

How to get everything done by doing it tomorrow

1 Put all the work that you are behind on in backlog folders (email, paper, etc.) and put it where you can't see it.
2 Collect all your incoming work during the day and deal with it in one batch the following day. Group together similar activities like email, paper, phone calls and tasks. Aim to clear the lot every day.
3 If anything is too urgent to leave to the following day, write it down on a separate list and action it at a convenient time during the day. Never take even the simplest action without writing it down first.
4 Spend some time on clearing the contents of the backlog folder(s) first thing every day. When you've finally cleared them, find something else you want to get sorted and start doing that first thing every day instead.

If you follow this simple process you will be totally on top of new work by tomorrow and you will be well on your way to clearing your backlog.

This book will tell you much more about how to do this, but the method essentially consists of these four steps.

1

What This Book Is About

To complain about a shortage of time is like a fish in the sea complaining that it has a shortage of water.

This book is about getting you to be 100 per cent creative, ordered and effective.

In my first two books I explored some very different ways of overcoming the problem of how we control our work and our time. In *Get Everything Done and Still Have Time to Play* I looked at the problems of the traditional methods of time management and then examined some better ways. In *How to Make Your Dreams Come True* I tried to get away from the whole concept of managing time, and instead looked at how we can get our goals to pull us towards them.

Both my books got a good reception from many people. Nevertheless, inevitably the ideas in them have done little to affect society at large. The problems and pressures of modern life are still there and if anything the pressures we put ourselves under at work have got even worse. Just the other day I received some questions from a journalist who was writing an article about time management. These are very typical of the sort of questions I get asked over and over again.

- I am always rushing. How can I stop?
- I always have to eat fast. How can I slow down?

- I am always having to multitask. How can I focus better?
- I always feel guilty about not spending more time with my family. What can I do about it?
- I never have time to exercise. How can I find the time?
- How can I find the time to take a holiday? I'm far too busy.

These are pretty common questions. The journalist was asking them because he believed the public would be interested in the answers, but they were also questions that he needed answering for himself.

These questions all imply that we have a shortage of time. Is this really true? Do we have a shortage of time? No, we don't. Time is the medium in which we exist. To complain about a shortage of time is like a fish in the sea complaining that it has a shortage of water. The next time that you complain that 'there aren't enough hours in the day', imagine for a moment that the day was lengthened to forty-eight hours. Would that enable you to be on top of your work? Not likely! You would almost certainly be just as behind as before.

It struck me as significant that the journalist found it necessary to ask me the questions that he did. They sounded like the inverse of the sort of advice that we give ourselves or our friends and family all the time. In fact his questions could easily be turned into simple rules for living:

- Don't rush.
- Take time to eat properly.
- Focus on one thing at a time.
- Make sufficient time for your family.

- Take adequate exercise.
- Go on regular holidays.

Really all that he and his readers have to do is to decide to keep to these rules, surely?

However, life is never as simple as that. What we decide to do and what we actually do are two different things. If you think of the decisions you have made over the past year, how many of them have been satisfactorily carried to a conclusion or are progressing properly to that end? If you are like most people, you will have acted on some of your decisions, I'm sure. But I'm also sure that a large proportion will have fallen by the wayside.

So a simple decision such as to take time to eat properly is in fact very difficult to carry out. Our new rule may work for a few days or a few weeks, but it won't be long before the pressures of work force us to make an exception to it. Before many days are up the exception will have become the rule and we are right back where we started. However much we rationalise the reasons why our decision didn't get carried out, we know deep in the heart of us that it was not really the circumstances that were to blame. We secretly acknowledge that there is something missing from our ability to carry out a decision once we have made it.

In fact if we are honest it sometimes feels as if it is easier to get other people to do what we want them to do than it is to get *ourselves* to do what we want to do. We like to think of ourselves as a sort of separate entity sitting in our body controlling it, but when we look at the way we behave most of the time that is not really the case. The body controls itself most of the time. We have a delusion of control. That's what it is – a delusion.

If we want to see how little control we have over ourselves, all most of us have to do is to look in the mirror. You might like to do that now. Ask yourself as you look at your image:

- Is my health the way I want it to be?
- Is my fitness the way I want it to be?
- Is my weight the way I want it to be?
- Is the way I am dressed the way I want it to be?

I am not asking you here to assess what sort of body you were born with, but what you have made of it and how good a state of repair you are keeping it in.

It may be that you are healthy, fit, slim and well-dressed. In which case have a look round at the state of your office or workplace:

- Is it as well organised as you want it to be?
- Is it as tidy as you want it to be?
- Do all your office systems (filing, invoicing, correspondence, etc.) work the way you want them to work?

If so, then you probably don't need to be reading this book.

I've just asked you to look at two aspects of your life that are under your direct control and are very little influenced by outside factors. If these things which are solely affected by you are not the way you want them to be, then in what sense can you be said to be in control at all?

A lot of this difficulty is due to the way our brains are organised. We have the illusion that we are a single person who acts in a 'unified' way. But it takes only a little reflection (and examination of our actions, as above) to realise that this is not the case at all. Our brains are made up of numerous different parts which deal with different things and often have different agendas.

I am now going to make a gross oversimplification and say that we have a rational brain and a reactive brain. This is not really a very scientific description, but talking about two brains in this way is useful for the practical purposes of managing our time. For a start, it helps us to understand why we have so much difficulty with implementing decisions.

You can imagine the rational brain as being like a government agency busy drawing up plans and regulations which it intends to impose on the rest of the body. It has all sorts of ideas about business expansion, family welfare, exercise and healthy eating, just to name a few. As with most government agencies, the plans work fine until they come up against reality.

In the case of the internal workings of the brain, the reality that the rational brain's plans come up against is the reactive brain. Imagine the reactive brain as a lizard sitting on a rock in the sun. If it sees a threat, such as a predator, it scuttles under the rock and freezes. If it sees a juicy bug which has strayed too close, it will snap it up. It doesn't have to think about it. It acts as a pre-programmed reaction. It really doesn't care that much at all about the rational brain's plans. The only thing it cares about is whether they constitute a threat or a nice juicy bug.

This part of the brain is hugely important for our survival. Can you imagine using rational thought processes

5

to avoid running over a child who runs out in front of your car? You need a quick reaction to an immediate threat. This is fundamental.

However, when it comes to making decisions and plans it is the rational brain that we should be using. If we run our days on the basis of the reactive brain, our work will consist of reacting to one stimulus after another. Come to think of it, that is quite a good description of how many people do in fact run their days. They are constantly fire-fighting, rushing from one thing to another, unable to keep their attention on anything long enough to think it through. The reactive brain is not a good work master.

Whenever we get a conflict between the rational brain and the reactive brain, the reactive brain usually wins because it is the stronger. We can make our plans about taking exercise every day, but there will come a day when it's too cold or raining too hard. The reactive brain regards this as a threat, and our rational plan goes out of the window. Or we decide to go on a diet and make rational decisions about what we can and cannot eat. But along comes a piece of chocolate cake and our reactive brain couldn't care less what our rational brain thinks – it snaps it up like a very juicy bug!

You may be wondering by now how anyone ever succeeds in getting fit or losing weight or carrying out any sort of rational plan. Obviously people do, so the reactive brain doesn't have things its own way the whole time. The reason why it doesn't is that the rational brain has one great advantage over the reactive brain – it is intelligent and the reactive brain isn't.

This means that the rational brain can work out

strategies to control the reactive brain – just as the government puts in a whole structure of inspectors, police, law courts, form-filling, officials and so forth to ensure the implementation of its plans. No one would take the slightest notice of anything the government said without this structure.

Success at a project is very rarely a matter of 'willpower'. It's usually a matter of having set up a good structure to support the carrying out of the project. Your project needs the mental and physical equivalents of the government's controlling structures. And just as no one would take any notice of the government without the structure, so your reactive brain won't take the slightest notice of your rational brain's plans without its structures to keep it under control.

There are all sorts of ways one can set up these structures. I will be exploring some in this book, but in reality there is no limit to the possibilities. What one is always aiming for is to make it easier to do the right thing than the wrong one. Is it easier for you to fill in your tax return than not to fill it in? Obviously in the natural way of things, it's much easier not to fill it in. But the government has put a structure in place that would make it very difficult for you not to fill it in – whether you like it or not! In the long run it is easier to fill it in; and that's what most of us eventually do, however unwillingly.

One of the key areas in which the rational brain needs to be able to control the reactive brain is the area of resistance and procrastination. Resistance to doing a task is largely a matter of the reactive brain seeing the task as a threat. The rational brain can tell the reactive brain as much as it likes about how important it is to get the task done. So long as the reactive brain regards the task as a threat, it will keep the brakes firmly on.

The rational brain has to be subtle here and persuade the reactive brain that there is no threat. The easiest way to do this is for you to pretend to yourself that you are not going to do the task. Remember that the reactive brain is not intelligent, and is therefore not capable of fathoming out the strategies of the rational brain.

A phrase such as 'I'm not really going to write that report now, but I'll just get the file out' will cause the reactive brain to switch the resistance off. Since getting the file out on its own is not perceived as a threat, the reactive brain has no reason to maintain the feelings of resistance. Very often the result is that the entire report gets written.

This is just one way in which we can use the power of the rational brain to work out strategies to control the reactive brain. Our aim is not to get rid of the reactive brain, but to ensure that both parts of the brain are working together rather than fighting each other. In the above example we started with a conflict: the rational brain had the intention of writing the report, while the reactive brain was resisting it as a threat. Once the resistance was switched off, both the rational brain and the reactive brain were freed to co-operate in the writing of the report.

If we were able to do this – to get the reactive brain to co-operate all the time in the plans made by the rational brain, we would be able to carry out the decisions that we make much more consistently than most of us do at the moment. Our ideal sequence would be Thought – Decision – Action. It would mean that our rational brain was controlling all the other parts of the brain to produce the desired result.

This would mean that every day we could plan out what we should do according to the best ways of achieving our goals and then carry out these actions as directly and effectively as possible. Of course some people do this already, and if you are one of them then you really don't need to be reading this book.

Unfortunately, for most of us the rational brain doesn't know the best strategies to control the reactive brain. We therefore tend to rely on willpower alone. This never works because the ideal sequence above is opposed by a stronger and more primitive one: Stimulus – Reaction. Without the right structures to keep it under control, Stimulus – Reaction will always tend to overwhelm Thought – Decision – Action.

Not knowing the right structures therefore means that we are left at the mercy of random stimuli. In spite of all the highly rational decisions that we make, it takes only one or two things to go wrong for our beautifully planned days to be reduced to chaos. We react like headless chickens to the random play of events during the day. One phone call, one crisis, one unexpected demand, and our plan for the day starts to wobble. A few more random events and the whole thing collapses like a pack of cards. No wonder many people give up on trying to plan their day altogether.

There is a good example of how this happens in my first book, *Get Everything Done and Still Have Time to Play*. I gave a preliminary exercise in that book which was intended to be a simple way of increasing mental strength, but has in fact proved too difficult for just about everyone who has tried it. I am sure there are people who have succeeded in the exercise – all I can say is that I have never come across anyone who has been able to do it for more than a few consecutive days!

The exercise is simplicity itself. If you would like to try it, all you have to do is pick one task which you are going to do the next day without fail, and then do it.

If you succeed at that task, then you pick another different task for the following day and make it just a little bit more difficult. And so you continue one day at a time, picking one task which you will do each day – each day a little bit more difficult. Once you are confident that you can carry out any task no matter how difficult without fail, you then repeat the process with two tasks.

It doesn't matter whether the tasks are meaningful or completely nonsensical. The idea is to do them for no other reason than because you have *decided* to do them.

Although the exercise sounds very simple and easy, it is in fact extremely difficult. Even if one starts off with a very simple task indeed on Day One (like moving a paper clip from one position on your desk to another), and moves by the slowest possible increments, it is almost impossible to keep going for a protracted time. The reason is that we will sooner or later get to a level of difficulty at which we are actively resisting the actions necessary to complete the task. In fact this is how we generally judge the difficulty of a proposed action – by how much we are resisting it rather than by how much skill or technical expertise it will take. This is why many people see doing their tax return as very difficult, even though no real skill is involved.

Another method I gave in the same book was the idea that one should do what one is resisting most. The problem I found with this is that one of two things happened. Either the mind fought back after a while and refused to do what was being resisted, or else one managed to persuade oneself that one was resisting the easiest and most trivial things.

My second book, *How to Make Your Dreams Come True*, took a very different look at how to manage one's time. Instead of dealing with mechanical systems for processing work, it dealt with getting one's goals to pull one towards them. It advised having a clear vision, dialoguing, and concentrating on what was going well. Although this worked well, there was a tendency among readers to think that they could realise their goals without having to do the fairly structured work on them that I recommended. The result was that they tended to drift rather than move purposely towards their goals.

As a result of writing these two books a few years ago, I have been almost continuously involved in giving seminars and working with individuals. I have developed many new insights and become even more aware of some of the problems that affect people. The result has been that I have developed methods that build on the previous books and go beyond them. It is these methods that I shall be sharing in the present book.

In the next chapter I will be looking at the principles that I have used in order to construct a new system of time management. I have found that there are some fundamental principles that are at the root of managing ourselves, and they form the basis of what I will be proposing. Every technique that I put forward in this book is an expression of one or more of these principles. They are:

Have a clear vision
One thing at a time

Little and often
Limits
Closed lists
Reduce randomness
Commitment v. interest

Test yourself

Which of the following situations are examples of Thought
– Decision – Action and which are examples of Stimulus –
Response?

1 You get back to the office from being out at a client
   meeting and check your emails to see what has arrived
   while you have been out. You deal with a couple that
   seem urgent, plus a few one-liners. Then you leave the
   rest for later.
2 A client phones you and asks you to get her some
   information. You promise you will get straight back to
   her.
3 You are an assistant in a shoe shop. You serve a
   customer who wants to try on some shoes.
4 A friend sends you an email telling you about a great
   new website. You click on the link and have a look at
   it.
5 Your assistant brings in some letters for you to sign.
   You deal with them immediately so that she can get
   them into the post.
6 Your boss dumps a load of work on your desk and
   says she needs it back by the end of the day. You feel
   a sense of panic, as you already have more than you
   can cope with.

7 You are a member of the fire service. An emergency call comes in and your team responds to it.

8 You come back from holiday to find 800 emails sitting in your computer. You spend several hours clearing the lot.

Answers

1 This is a classic Stimulus – Response. You have reacted to the emails that caught your attention and have left the rest for an unspecified time in the future. This is the way to ensure that you will have a backlog of email.

2 Stimulus – Response. You are interrupting whatever you were doing to go on a search for information for your client. There's no mention of whether it is really urgent or not.

3 Thought – Decision – Action. A shop is organised to make an immediate response to customers. This is a matter of planning and organisation, not reaction.

4 Stimulus – Response. There is absolutely no reason why you need to check the website immediately – unless of course you are trying to avoid doing some work!

5 Thought – Decision – Action. You have presumably arranged for your secretary to bring in letters for signature at a specific time each day. This is a matter of planning and organisation.

6 Stimulus – Response on both your and your boss's part. Your boss has probably panicked because she has been sitting on the work for weeks. You are panicking instead of planning rationally how to deal with the extra work.

7 Thought – Decision – Action. The fire service is organised to respond to emergencies in a planned and systematic way.

8 Thought – Decision – Action. Contrast this with Question 1. This is a planned decision to clear *all* the emails, not a haphazard trawl through them.

2

The Principles

A clear vision is as much about what you are not going to do as it is about what you are going to do.

Have a clear vision
One thing at a time
Little and often
Limits
Closed lists
Reduce randomness
Commitment v. interest
What do we need?

First principle

Have a clear vision

My first principle is to have a clear vision. Of course there is nothing new about stressing the importance of having a vision – it features in just about every self-help or business book. Everyone these days has a vision. In fact the 'vision statement' has become almost a cliché in the business world. But it's also a cliché that most firms' vision statements are pretty meaningless. I suspect that applies to most individuals' vision statements too. Many people and organisations have a vision, but how many have a *clear* vision?

The aim of a vision is to bring clarity and focus. If it

doesn't do that, then it is worse than useless. Does it really give clarity for a firm to have a vision statement like 'We intend to be the market leader in our field' – especially if all its competitors have the same vision statement? What on earth does it matter who is the market leader anyway, unless the purpose of the business is to build as grandiose an empire as possible? In which case, it might be more honest to say so. I doubt, though, that 'We intend to build as grandiose an empire as possible' would go down very well with the shareholders. We may think, however, that this is the vision that many organisations seem in practice to be working to.

So if we are not careful, instead of bringing clarity, our vision statements can act as a smokescreen. The question we should always be asking ourselves is, 'What am I/are we actually trying to achieve?' It is a question to be asked just as much – perhaps more – when sitting down to write a letter of complaint, as when setting out the strategy for a multimillion-pound investment.

The clearer you are about your vision, the more likely you are to achieve it. Your vision should bring your efforts sharply into focus, not envelop everything in a soft-focus fuzz. This usually means defining it as narrowly as possible.

A clear vision is as much about what you are *not* going to do as it is about what you *are* going to do. It must establish the limits to your action. When you are in a restaurant and give your order to the waiter, you are saying 'no' to everything else on the menu. In the same way, when you decide on a course of action you should not only be choosing it but also rejecting all the alternative courses of action.

Exercise

Instead of writing a to-do list for tomorrow's work, try writing a list of things you are *not* going to do instead. To give a few examples:

- I am not going to answer the phone until after 11 a.m.
- I am not going to work through lunch.
- I am not going to work later than 6 p.m.
- I am not going to work on any project except Project X.
- I am not going to spend more than half an hour on my email.
- I will confine myself to the items on my action list until I have completed them.

Much of the trouble we have with managing our time is because we don't establish proper limits on our work. If we attempt to do every possible task during the course of a day, it is inevitable that we are going to have a fractured and unfocused day. We need to select the metaphorical meal that we can eat without giving ourselves indigestion.

Second principle

One thing at a time

The first principle – have a clear vision – leads logically into my second principle: do one thing at a time. The worst thing you can do is to spread your efforts and your focus over too many things. You must establish proper limits on your current work, and the most important limit to put in place is that you should be working on only one thing at any one time.

In the last section I wrote about being in a restaurant

and in effect saying no to everything on the menu except the current meal that you wish to eat. We have no problem doing that in a restaurant because we know that we are physically unable to eat more than one main course – and anyway it would cost far too much to eat everything. Yet when it comes to selecting a 'meal' of things to work on from the menu of life, we seem to be incapable of not trying to eat far more than we are capable of. As the old saying goes, 'Our eyes are bigger than our stomachs'. Just as we are physically unable to eat too large a meal, we are physically unable to do all the things we have taken on. And it is likely to prove extremely expensive too.

Tackling one thing at a time, getting it right and then moving on to the next thing, has always been the way that successful people have advanced. It doesn't matter how you define success. We tend to think unsuccessful people are unsuccessful because they sit around doing nothing. But it's often for quite the opposite reason: they take on far too much – all sorts of wonderful projects at the same time – and never bring any of them to fruition.

Of course no one's life is so simple that they can literally concentrate on one thing to the exclusion of all else. There's all the routine stuff that needs to be done on a daily or weekly basis. This needs to be kept firmly in its place with a good system to handle it so that it supports your main endeavour rather than getting in its way. If routine work is handled well by simple and effective systems, your creativity and imagination can be directed accurately to where they need to be without distraction.

Most of the rest of this book is about how to make use of this principle to focus on doing your day's work in a systematic way. For the time being, you might want to have a go at the following exercise so you can experience for yourself the power of doing one thing at a time.

Exercise

Take a sheet of paper and make a list of all the things you intend to get around to some day. Include your work and your private life. Don't include anything that you have to get done by a certain date. Ideally they should be the sort of things that won't get done at all unless you make a conscious resolve to do them.

Select one out of the list – the one you are going to get done first. To start off, you may want to make it something fairly small.

Once you have decided on the one, you need to make two resolutions. The first is that you are going to concentrate on this one project until it is complete. The second is that you will not touch any of the others until you have finished the first one.

You can run this exercise repeatedly. You may find that a lot of things succeed in getting done!

Third principle

Little and often

My next principle is that the human mind works most effectively when it is doing something little and often. This is a principle that is well known in the fields of education and training, but it applies just as much in the world of work too.

If you have a report to write or a project to complete, the best way is to work on it little and often rather than in occasional great bursts of action.

The same applies if you are trying to learn an instrument or a foreign language. If you have lessons once a week, your teacher will tell you not to save all your homework up until the night before but to do a little every day.

It applies to the body as well as to the mind – the best way to get fit is to take exercise little and often. If you do nothing for weeks and then take a huge amount of exercise in one go you are very likely to damage yourself.

The reason the mind likes to work this way is that it has time to assimilate, make connections and get new insights. You have probably noticed if you leave a bit of work overnight that when you come back to it you seem to have moved on with it. You have some new insights or a difficult bit has now become easier.

An example of this principle would be the writing of articles, reports and even books. Many people tackle this sort of task by attempting to write the whole thing in one go from beginning to end. This has several disadvantages. The size of the task makes it seem daunting, and it's only too easy to build up a lot of resistance to it. It also doesn't give the mind time to develop what it being written.

In the old days we didn't have much choice about this because it took far too long to type repeated drafts or, even worse, write everything out several times in longhand. Nowadays we have word processors, and we can use them to make our life much easier. It is now very easy to write a series of rapid drafts, in which the material gets amplified and refined in each draft.

When I first learnt the technique of writing in a series of rapid drafts, my first draft would usually consist of nothing more than a few words jotted down. My second draft would add a bit more and I would go on revising it until I had it in the form I wanted.

There are two great advantages to doing it this way. First of all it gets rid of the perfectionist feeling that it has to be got right first time. If I think a sentence is a bit clumsy, what does it matter? There'll be another draft along in a moment. The second advantage is that engaging with the material in this way allows new thoughts and insights to appear.

As an example, here is the first draft of the first two chapters of this book. As you can see, it consists of little more than a few thoughts in no very logical order. It took me no more than a couple of minutes to write.

Previous books
Get Everything Done and Still Have Time to Play
How to Make Your Dreams Come True
Preliminary exercise
Too difficult
Resistance principle
Basic principles
One thing at a time
Little and often
Limits
Closed lists
Reducing randomness

I then wrote a second draft which took a bit longer, but not much. You can see how ideas and thoughts are beginning to be filled in.

Some time since wrote previous books

Not much has changed about the pressures we put ourselves under

Work stress

Lack of balance

Not able to act the way we want to

The way the brain is organised

Ideal world make decision and carry it out without fail

Many (most) of our decisions never get carried out. Why?

Thought – Decision – Action

Reactive part of our mind is stronger than rational part

I gave a preliminary exercise in *Get Everything Done and Still Have Time to Play* which has proved too difficult

Intended to build mental strength – instead shown how difficult to do what decided

No one succeeded in doing it!

Resistance principle

Tends to degrade – resisting trivia

Many thoughts and insights come in last four years

Basic principles have become clearer

One thing at a time

  Focus

Little and often

  The way the mind works

  Good example first draft of this chapter

  Previous books

  Get Everything Done and Still Have Time to Play

  How to Make Your Dreams Come True

  Preliminary exercise

  Too difficult

  Resistance principle

  Basic principles

One thing at a time
Little and often
Limits
Closed lists
Reducing randomness
Limits
Shakespeare's sonnets
Make it easier to focus
Examples: menu of life, end effect, closed lists
Closed lists
Powerful tool
Reducing randomness
Main problem with organising day
Anything we can do to reduce it will make huge difference
Where do random things come from?
Threats and pleasures (like lizard on rock)

Five drafts later I reached the form that you are reading now. If you compare this outline with the final version you will be able to see how my ideas have developed and evolved during the writing.

Fourth principle

Define your limits
We've already talked about a clear goal or vision being as much about what we are *not* going to do as about what we *are* going to do. This is an example of another way that the human mind likes to work. Our creativity expresses itself best when it is working in the confines of very closely defined limits. In spite of what many teachers

of 'creative thinking' say, the best way to be creative is not to try to think without limits but to very carefully define what those limits should be. It is much easier to focus once clear limits have been set.

Many articles and books on creativity encourage us to 'think out of the box' and get rid of all the restrictions on our thinking. The trouble with this advice is that it is almost entirely wrong. It is very difficult to be creative when 'anything goes' and you have no limitations, because it is the limitations that actually encourage creativity.

Give your mind a focused problem and it will respond. If I ask you to come up with a revolutionary new idea for improving motor cars in general, the best you could probably come up with would be a few vague suggestions. Yet if I asked you to think of a way of improving the steering wheel in your own car, you could almost certainly come up with some very useful ideas. The more focused the problem, the easier it is to be creative with it.

A good example is rhyme and metre in poetry. Consider the following poem, one of perhaps the greatest collection of poems in the world – Shakespeare's *Sonnets*.

No longer mourn for me when I am dead
Than you shall hear the surly sullen bell
Give warning to the world that I am fled
From this vile world with vilest worms to dwell:
Nay, if you read this line, remember not
The hand that writ it, for I love you so,
That I in your sweet thoughts would be forgot,
If thinking on me then should make you woe.
O! if, I say, you look upon this verse,

When I perhaps compounded am with clay,
Do not so much as my poor name rehearse;
But let your love even with my life decay;
Lest the wise world should look into your moan,
And mock you with me after I am gone.

In writing this poem, was Shakespeare hampered by the fact that he had chosen to use a very conventional format, in which not only are the metre and rhyming scheme fixed, but also to some extent the subject matter? No, not at all. He produced a great work of art by the very fact that he was exploring the limitations of the format. And not only did he do it once, he did it over a hundred and fifty times – each time producing a different effect!

What has all this got to do with us in our daily lives? Well, have a think about your life. Are you working on clearly focused objectives with clearly defined boundaries? Or are your life and work diffused over many poorly defined projects with no clear boundaries? Which is likely to produce the greater degree of creativity in your life?

If you have the feeling that you are getting nowhere or that you can't keep your impetus going, the reason is very likely to be poorly defined limits. The cure is to narrow your life down and define it more closely. You will find paradoxically that you are able to exercise far more freedom within your narrow boundaries, than the deceptive 'freedom' that has no focus, no boundaries and is ultimately unsatisfying because it is going nowhere.

Another example of the way in which establishing limits can improve the way the mind works is limits of time. You are much more likely to be able to work in a concentrated way on a task if you are given a definite period of time in which to accomplish it.

If you want to work in a really concentrated way on a major task, then try working in timed bursts. You can find by experience what length suits you or the task best. It might be an hour or it might be twenty minutes. In the early stages of a high-resistance task it might even be five minutes. If you know that you are going to stop working on the task at a precise point of time, you will find that you are able to concentrate on it much more than if you are working on it for as long as you feel like it. I will deal some more with timed bursts in Chapter 13, Keeping Going.

Another aspect of using limits is the closed list, which is my next principle.

Fifth principle

Closed lists

A closed list is any list that has a line drawn at the bottom so nothing can be added to it. This is in contrast with an open list, which can be constantly added to. It is much easier to work with a closed list rather than an open list.

There are several reasons for this. The most important is that closing a list enables all the items on it to be dealt with without the distraction of new work being added. The list acts as a buffer between you and distractions.

Another important characteristic of closed lists is that once the list has been closed it cannot get any larger. It can only stay the same size or get smaller. In fact it has a natural tendency to get smaller because some of the items on the list may become outdated or no longer relevant.

Also note that, provided you are going to clear the whole list, it does not matter what order you do the items in.

The exercise that I am going to give you on page 40 is an example of a closed list. You start the day with a closed list of items which you have to complete in order to earn your points for the day. One thing you may discover if you tackle this exercise seriously is that it is easier to deal with the items on the list than it is to deal with the rest of your work. This is particularly noticeable if you refuse to do anything else until you have finished the list. This is because the rest of your work is open-ended, in other words an open list.

The prime example of an open list is the traditional to-do list. What makes it an open list is the fact that you can add items to it as you go along. This adds to the phenomenon of randomness, which I will deal with in the next section.

A good example of a closed list is when you deal with your email in batches at regular intervals rather than piecemeal as it comes in during the day. If you do this, you will find that it is much quicker and more efficient to clear a batch of emails completely than to allow yourself to be continuously distracted by individual emails throughout the day.

Another example of the closed list is a checklist. When you break a task down into its component parts and make a checklist, you are making it easier to do the task. Note that making a detailed checklist in this way does not add to the amount of work you have to do. In fact it will probably save you work. A good example of this sort of checklist is a list of things to be done by a mechanic servicing a car.

The concept of the closed list – whether in the form of a batch or a checklist – is a powerful tool that can be exploited in many ways. The title of this book, *Do It Tomorrow*, refers to one way of making a closed list. This forms a major part of the systematic way of dealing with work that makes up the heart of this book.

Open list	Closed list
New items can be added	Nothing new can be added
Tends to grow	Tends to get smaller
Sequence is important	Sequence doesn't matter
Relatively difficult to clear	Relatively easy to clear
Demotivating	Motivating

To experience the power of the closed list over an open list, you can use the closed list principle to deal with backlogs of work. Many people have great difficulty clearing a backlog. However hard they work away at it, it seems to fill up with new stuff just as fast as they clear it. The problem here is that the backlog is open. The solution is to close it. In order to do so you can use the following sequence:

Step 1 – Isolate the backlog
You need to get the backlog out of the way so that you can't see it any longer. With a backlog of email you can open a folder called 'Backlog' and move the entire contents of your inbox into it. Suddenly you have an empty inbox – bliss!

If your backlog is paper, then gather all the paper

together and put it in a folder called 'Backlog'. If a folder isn't big enough then use a box (in extreme cases I have known people use an entire room!).

You can use the same principle with any other type of backlog. The aim is to close off the backlog and isolate it from new stuff coming in.

Step 2 – Get the system for new stuff right

You can't deal with the backlog until you have got the system right for dealing with new stuff coming in. Otherwise all you are going to succeed in doing is to build up further backlogs. Ask yourself, 'If my backlog was completely clear, would I be able to keep it that way?' If the answer is 'no' then you have got to look at how you are dealing with your work. It is pointless dealing with the backlog until this is sorted out. Using the principles I have already mentioned, the easiest way of dealing with emails, paper, etc., is by batches. I will be giving detailed instructions in the rest of this book on how to do this.

One of the reasons backlogs build up in the first place is that we attract far too much inessential stuff. Chuck junk mail in the rubbish without even opening it. Cancel subscriptions for newsletters you don't read. Don't write off for things you don't need. Keep asking yourself, 'Why am I receiving this?' If you have too high a volume of stuff to deal with, keep looking at ways of pruning it.

Step 3 – Get rid of the backlog

If you have done Steps 1 and 2 correctly, your backlog can now only get smaller. You don't need to try to get rid of the lot in one go. You can keep chipping away at it. With emails, try clearing one day at a time, starting with the oldest. With paper, try clearing it one subject at a time – such as all bank statements, then all bills, then all client letters and so forth. There are all sorts of ways of dealing with a backlog, and it doesn't really matter which one you use. As I've already pointed out, even if you don't make any effort to deal with the backlog it will tend to get smaller of its own accord.

Sixth principle

Reducing random factors

If I ask a group of people what the main thing is that stops them from completing their work during the day, the most common answer will inevitably be 'interruptions'. What this means is that they are allowing random factors to disrupt their plans for the day.

We will never be completely successful in eliminating random factors because life just isn't that predictable. But it is enormously important to keep them as few as possible because of the adverse effects they bring with them.

Every time we do something that wasn't in our plan for the day, we have allowed a random factor to come in and disrupt our work. It doesn't matter what it is – it means that we are doing something that we didn't plan to do. This might not be a problem if we still succeed in doing the things that we did plan to do, but this is seldom the case. Usually what happens is that we fail to do several of the planned actions. Unfortunately these tend to be the more difficult or challenging actions – precisely the ones that it is most important for us to be doing, in fact.

Random factors are the real killers for a day's work. A lot

of random input into our day means that our day starts to run us rather than us running it. There are various degrees of randomness. All days are virtually bound to have some randomness, but some people allow their days to run almost entirely at random. Most people have at least some semblance of a plan, written or mental, but they often don't succeed in keeping to it because so many things come in and have to be dealt with randomly. The result is that what they intend to do during the day and what they actually do are two completely different things.

We can never entirely get away from random elements in our day, but the more we can eliminate them the more we will be able to control our day. Random things come from all sorts of different sources, such as our clients, our boss, our subordinates, our colleagues and indeed ourselves. What we tend to do with random elements is react to them; that is, we use the reactive part of our brain. Some we react to as threats and some as pleasures. We need to learn how to use rational brains to control them and reduce the disruption they bring to a minimum.

The real problem with randomness is that things tend to get done or not done almost exclusively according to how much they attract our attention – in other words, how much noise they are making. Of all the ways open to us for prioritising our work, prioritising by noise is probably the least sensible!

Test yourself

Which of these situations introduces a random factor into your day?

1 You are a member of the fire service. You have to answer an emergency call with your team for a big fire that has broken out.

2 Your boss summons you into his office and gives you a new project to work on. It is going to involve a lot of work over the next few weeks.

3 A friend sends you an email asking you to take a look at a brilliant new internet site. You click on the link and spend some time evaluating it.

4 A client calls with an urgent request that you have to attend to immediately.

5 Your boss gives you some work which she wants on her desk by close of play today.

6 You have been sitting on some work for a couple of weeks. You give it to your assistant with a request that he action it today.

7 You have to go out and get some more milk for the office fridge because yet again no one remembered to bring any in with them this morning.

Answers

1 Answering emergency calls is your job. So this is not a random factor. You are organised to respond to these calls. Big fires may be random occurrences but you are not dealing with them in a random way.

2 The interview with your boss is a random factor, but

the work coming out of it is not. You have been given a project to work on over several weeks, so you can plan it and carry it out in a non-random way.

3 This is a completely random distraction and you allowed it in – quite unnecessarily!

4 Yes, this is a random factor. However, you do need to be very clear about what constitutes 'an urgent request'. Rushing around at your clients' beck and call may not be the best way to do business. If your job consists of responding immediately to client requests, then you need to be properly organised to do so – in which case it ceases to be random.

5 This is a random factor and a very disruptive one. If your boss does this a lot you need to challenge her about it.

6 This is terrible. You are finally getting round to doing in a random way something that you should have done ages ago in a planned way. Even worse, you are also guilty of inflicting a completely unnecessary random factor on one of your subordinates. This is one of the worst time-management crimes a boss can commit!

7 This is pathetic – lack of planning and system leading to a random disruption.

Seventh principle

Commitment v. interest

Consider the difference between these two statements:

'I'm interested in writing.'
'I'm committed to getting a regular column in my local newspaper.'

What images do they conjure up? If you were talking to someone you'd just met and they said to you, 'I'm interested in writing', would you regard it as anything out of the ordinary? Sometimes I think that just about everyone I've ever met is interested in writing. It seems to be one of the most common pipe dreams that people have – and a pipe dream is what it usually remains. When you hear people say about someone, 'He has a lot of interests', you usually get the impression that the person has a fairly superficial knowledge of a lot of disconnected subjects without having achieved very much in any of them.

You wouldn't for instance expect anyone to say:

> 'Beethoven was interested in music.'
> 'Shakespeare was interested in writing plays.'
> 'David Beckham is interested in football.'

If someone tells you that they are committed to something, that gives a very different impression. It gives you the impression that they live, breathe and eat the subject. When you hear people say about someone, 'She's committed herself to that charity project', you know that you need to keep well out of that person's way if you don't want to find yourself being persuaded to get out your cheque book!

When people come to me for coaching, they often tell me about their interests. Most people have quite a collection of unrelated interests, and, of course, one interest keeps getting in the way of another. There is no real upper limit to the number of things that someone can be interested in. Nothing very much is likely to come of any of them unless interest turns into commitment. So one of the early steps in the coaching process is to see what the person is prepared to commit themselves to.

The problem with commitments is that it is possible to have only a very limited number of them. Yes, the word was 'limited' – we are back again to the question of limits. Commitments imply exclusion. If we are really committed to one thing it implies that we are excluding everything else that might conflict with that commitment.

Now I am not saying that there is anything wrong with having interests. A person without any interests would be very dull. But it is immensely important to distinguish between having an interest in something and having a commitment to something. It is commitment that will make the real difference in your life and work.

Knowing what your commitments are is an essential part of making decisions. We make decisions all the time – at every hour of the day. If we don't have a commitment to act as a signpost to help us in the making of decisions, we have nothing on which to base them. Our decisions, like our actions, will tend to be random.

Often when making day-to-day decisions we come up against the rational and reactive brains pulling in opposite directions. This usually presents itself as a conflict between immediate gratification and long-term gain. For example:

- I want to be slim but I also want to eat a slice of chocolate cake.
- I want to be out of debt but I also want to buy that new DVD recorder.
- I want to write my book but I also want to watch the television.

The question to ask yourself here is: 'How will I feel once I've done it?'

- How will you feel when you are slim?
- How will you feel after you've eaten the slice of chocolate cake and your weight has soared?
- How will you feel when you're out of debt?
- How will you feel when you've splurged on a new DVD recorder and you have even more debt?
- How will you feel when you've written your book?
- How will you feel when you've spent your time watching television and your book is still a pipe dream?

This is where commitment counts!

Exercise

Make a list of all the things you are interested in doing. Don't write down anything that you have already fully committed to doing. They should be things that you've thought about doing but which you have at the most only made an occasional stab at. Some typical things that people write down when they do this exercise are:

- Losing weight
- Yoga
- Getting fit
- Running my own business
- Doing some charity work
- Learning French/Spanish/Japanese/any other language
- Getting a higher degree or qualification
- Changing my job

Make the list as long as you can. Now ask yourself which of these you might be prepared to make a commitment to – that is to say a commitment to carrying it through to completion. Cross the items off the list to which you couldn't see yourself making a serious commitment.

Once you've refined your list, ask yourself for each of the remaining items:

- What would I need to *start* doing in order to commit myself fully to it?
- What would I need to *stop* doing in order to commit myself fully to it?
- Would I be prepared to pay the price necessary for full commitment to this item?

Once you have faced up to what would be needed for full commitment to each remaining item, you can now decide whether you are in fact going to commit yourself to one or more of the items.

What do we need?

Now that we've looked at these seven principles of good time management, can we find a way of using all of them in a systematic manner? Is it possible to put something better in place of the random, fractured nature of so many of our days?

In the next chapter we will look at what we might be able to do if we could find a better system. In the meantime here are a couple of exercises to help you experience the reality of what I have been saying.

Exercise 1

This is an exercise to assess how much randomness you currently have in your day. First make a list of what you actually intend to do tomorrow (or your next full working day). Don't include scheduled items such as appointments, meetings, etc. Work out how much unscheduled work time you have and decide exactly what you intend to do during that time. Draw a line at the bottom of the list.

Tomorrow, work through the list and cross off as many items as you can. But here's the important bit – during the course of the day write down below the line anything you do that was not on the original list. It's very easy to fool yourself here, so make sure you include everything – conversations with friends and colleagues, daydreaming, surfing the net, sending text messages, responding to impulses.

The purpose of the exercise is to give you a feel for how much control you are currently exercising over your day. At the end of the day you should be able to see clearly how much of your original list you were able to do and also how many random items were introduced into your day. Ask yourself the following questions:

1 What percentage of the items on the *original list* did I succeed in doing?
2 Looking at what I actually did during the day, what percentage of tasks were on the *original list* and what percentage were *added* during the day?
3 How many things did I do during the day *without* writing them down?

Here's a simplified example. Peter writes out a list of the things he plans to do tomorrow:

Clear email
Finish report
Book flights for American conference
Arrange interview with new staff member
Buy new diary
Call Jane about next week
Investigate new suppliers
Learn how to use new software package

By the end of the day Peter has cleared his email, arranged the interview, bought the diary and called Jane. But he has not finished the report, booked the flights or investigated new suppliers. So he has completed four out of the seven tasks, which represents 57 per cent.

He also did quite a few things that were not on the original list. The items that he wrote below the line were:

Investigate problem for client
Read important email attachment
Sort out crisis in accounts department
Tidy collapsed pile of books

So altogether Peter actioned eight items that he wrote down, of which four were on his original list and four were written in during the day. This means that his day was 50 per cent random.

But in fact this paints much too rosy a picture because he never got around to writing down the various conversations he had with colleagues, the time he spent reading the newspaper and the half-hour he spent researching holiday destinations on the Internet. So in fact the ratio between planned items and unplanned items among Peter's actions was considerably worse than 50:50.

The problem that this amount of random activity causes is that it's not just what gets done that is random – what *doesn't* get done is random too. This means that whether something gets done or not is as much a matter of chance as of rational decision.

Exercise 2

This next exercise is also designed to make you more aware of how much or how little you are actually in control of your day. By making you more aware it should also help you to improve your control.

The exercise consists of a daily challenge in which you compete against yourself to score as many points as possible each day.

To score points, you have to decide the previous day how many points you are going to attempt to score the following day. Then you write down a list comprising that number of tasks. So, for example, if you decide you want to try to score three points the following day, you write down a list of three tasks. So you might write down:

1 Buy new calculator.
2 Call my sister.
3 Mow the lawn.

The tasks should be simple and specific so that at the end of the day you have either done them or you haven't. Then you score one point for each completed task.

That sounds easy enough, doesn't it? But there's a catch. You score the points only if you complete every item on the list that day. If you haven't completed every item, then you score no points at all for that day – no excuses accepted!

Please note that you score no points for doing things that are not on your list. This is extremely important, as we shall see later in the book.

This exercise makes us face up to what we are habitually not doing when we draw up our to-do lists or plans for the day. We don't draw up our list of things to do in the expectation of completing it. In fact we would be quite surprised if we did. The result is that our days are poorly planned and at the mercy of random factors.

Use this exercise to see how many items you can work up to. Start with just a few – possibly even one – and keep working at the exercise day by day until you can write quite a long list and still be sure of finishing it. You may find it much more difficult than you expect. The key is to do the items on the list first thing – before you embark on the rest of the day's work.

Remember those questions the journalist asked me in Chapter 1? Now that you have read the principles that I have just given and tried out some of the exercises, you might be interested in the answers that I gave to the journalist. Here they are. See if you can spot which of the principles of good time management have been used in the answers.

Q. I am always rushing. How can I stop?

A. You will have a much higher quality of work if you don't rush from one thing to another. Make sure that you are not overscheduled. Allow sufficient time between meetings for travel, preparation, etc. Also remember that the blank spaces in your schedule are not empty – they already contain all the work that you will have to do in your office!

Q. I always have to eat fast. How can I slow down?

A. Give yourself a proper lunch break during which you do nothing that is work-related. Give it a definite start and stop time, and keep to it. Breaks are very important for keeping yourself working at maximum effectiveness. You will find you get more done, not less, if you give yourself proper breaks.

Q. I am always having to multitask. How can I focus better?

A. It is quicker and more effective to do one thing at a time. Trying to do more than one thing at a time usually results in none of them being done properly. Plan your day carefully and stick to it. Do not allow new stuff to interrupt your plan unless it is absolutely essential.

Q. I always feel guilty about not spending more time with my family. What can I do about it?

A. Give yourself a definite finishing time in the evening and stick to it. Do not take work home and have at least one day a week on which you do no work at all. You will find that you get more done as a result of limiting yourself in this way because you will be able to maintain your concentration better during the day.

Q. I never have time to exercise. How can I find the time?

A. Remember the motto: 'Work hard, play hard.' Regard your personal time as just as important as your work time and give as much attention to planning it as you do to planning your work. What are you working *for* if you don't have a personal life?

Q. How can I find the time to take a holiday? I'm far too busy.

A. What do you mean, you don't have the time? Of course you do! You have 365 days a year in which you can go on vacation. Decide how many of those you are prepared to give up in order to do some work, and take the rest of the time off!

3

Creative, Ordered and Effective

Being well ordered has little to do with character; it has everything to do with how your life is structured.

As I said at the beginning of Chapter 1, this book is about getting you to be 100 per cent creative, ordered and effective. Let's have a look at what this entails.

The qualities of being creative, ordered and effective depend very closely on each other. You may be extremely creative, but if you aren't ordered as well you won't be effective. You will spend your time thinking up great ideas but never being able to make anything of them.

On the other hand your life can be wonderfully ordered, but if it doesn't contain any creativity it will be sterile, no more than coldly efficient. You may be one of those people who drive others mad because of your passion for keeping things in their place. You will never be effective because you are more concerned with how things look than with how they really are.

And finally it is impossible to be effective without both creativity and order. Effectiveness is not a quality on its own; rather it is a measure of how far the order in your life allows your creativity to express itself.

So, at the risk of oversimplifying things, here is a formula which expresses the relationship between these three qualities:

Effectiveness = Creativity x Order

Essentially, effectiveness is the difference between action and activity. Your working life can be full of hectic activity, but the amount of real action you take can be very small. Busyness and effectiveness are not the same thing by a long way.

This book is not a guide to being creative. I am assuming that you are already a talented and creative person. What I intend to do in this book is give you a step-by-step guide to liberating your creativity from the shackles of being disordered. You will find here directions on how to be totally in control of your life with the minimum of effort.

How can you possibly succeed in arriving at this? You may have been struggling for years against your inability to get ordered. And you may regard this as a deep character fault – something which is innate in you and which you cannot change.

Fortunately, nothing could be further from the truth. Being ordered has little to do with character; it has everything to do with how your life is structured. If you have a structure that makes it easier for you to do the right thing, then the right thing is what you will do.

Conversely, if you find yourself consistently doing the wrong thing, it is because the structure of your life is making it easier to do the wrong thing than the right thing. Change the structure and you will change the result.

You've probably already experienced the truth of this in your own life. Most people behave differently in different situations. You may be hopelessly untidy at home, but well organised at work, or vice versa. You may have been able to work in a concentrated way when you worked for a firm, but have found yourself constantly distracted since you started your own business. In both these cases you are the same person; only the structure is different.

Whenever you find that you are not acting in the way you want to, don't berate yourself for being a useless person. Look at how what you are doing is structured. Do you have a system for dealing with incoming emails that ensures that they get actioned quickly and efficiently, or do you have a system that ensures that half of them will get forgotten about? The system many people have for dealing with email is to cherry-pick the ones that stand out and leave the rest 'for later'. Is this a system that is going to ensure that all your email gets done effectively? I would suggest it isn't. In fact it's a system that will virtually ensure a backlog of email. What can you do about it? Change the system! If you get the structure right, everything else will come right too.

I will be giving many suggested ways in this book in which you can change the structure of what you are doing. But remember there is never only one way to do something. If you remember to apply the principle that different structures lead to different results, you can use your creativity to invent your own systems.

The methods that I am going to be teaching are very simple. They don't require years of learning or practice. They are the sort of things you can put into use during the course of an afternoon and find them having an immediate effect. In fact, I will give you a challenge – you can be completely organised twenty-four hours after reading this book! Does that sound possible? Well, I can assure you that it is in the sense that you can be completely on top of all your current work and have a workable plan for dealing with any backlogs of work that you may have.

Some people listen to my methods and their reaction is to say, 'That sounds great – I'll put it into practice just as soon as I've caught up with my work.' That's the wrong way to go about it. Put my methods into practice, and then you will be in a position to catch up with your work!

Where are you starting from?

Let's see where you are at the moment. Mark yourself out of ten for how creative you feel you are. This is a purely subjective judgment so don't spend a long time trying to work out the right answer – it's best to answer straight off the top of your head. Once you've done that, mark yourself out of ten for how ordered you feel you are.

Now multiply the two answers together and you have your percentage measure of how effective you are.

You can write the answers down here or on a separate piece of paper:

Creative_____ x Ordered _____

= _____ per cent Effective

For example, if you consider yourself to be very creative you might give yourself an eight. But at the same time you feel that you are rather disordered, so you give yourself a four for that quality. Multiplied together these give a score of thirty-two. That means that although you are a very creative person you are working at only 32 per cent effectiveness.

Now what someone in this position tends to do when

they feel their effectiveness is low is to try to work on raising their creativity. They may go on a course; they may aim for a qualification or a higher degree. This is all to the good, but note that however much work they do on their creativity they can only raise their creativity score to a maximum of ten. This would be a great achievement, of course, but how much would it change their effectiveness? Since they are still only 40 per cent ordered, their effectiveness will have increased only to 40 per cent. This is better than nothing, to be sure, but it's not a huge improvement.

On the other hand let's look at what happens if, instead of working on their creativity, they work on how ordered they are. If they were able to get themselves up to a ten for orderliness, they would be working at 80 per cent effectiveness. That's a huge increase, and achieved without having to gain any further qualifications or certifications. So it is clear that the greatest rewards will come from paying attention to getting ordered.

The above actually understates the effect of concentrating on order rather than creativity. This is because becoming more ordered is in itself likely to free up your creativity. So you might find that raising your score for how ordered you are also raises your score for creativity without your having to do anything specifically about it. So by working on your orderliness on its own, you might find that your effectiveness has risen to 85 per cent. A leap from 32 per cent effectiveness to 85 per cent effectiveness is really worth having.

For most people this doesn't work the other way round. Increasing your creativity is unlikely to make you more ordered.

The aim of this book is to raise your score for how ordered you are to ten out of ten. Well, maybe ten is a little too high to be aiming for – so let's say nine-and-a-half out of ten. How likely are you to succeed in that aim? That depends on how closely you follow the instructions!

When you know what it is that you want to achieve, and you have developed a strategy to keep your efforts focused on it, then you have a winning formula.

If people were really able to control their own lives, what would they be able to do?

They would be able to complete their work every day

When you stop work for the day, do you say to yourself, 'I've finished – I've done everything I had to do today'? In some types of job you can say that. But for most executive, managerial or entrepreneurial jobs the amount of work to do seems never-ending. The one thing you can be sure about is that the people in these jobs are never going to get to the end of their to-do lists. Nevertheless, by the time you finish this book you should know exactly what to do in order to get your day's work finished every day.

They would know what a day's work consists of so that they would know exactly when they have finished it

Before you can say that you have completed your work for the day, you need to know what it consists of. If you were to write down all the tasks you have outstanding, how much would it relate to one day's work? Probably not at all! Not only is the list almost certainly too long to be completed in one day, but the items on it have come in over a wide timeframe. Some tasks came up today, some yesterday, some a week or more ago, and there are usually a few lurking in the background which you have been putting off for months. So your list represents neither one day's worth of incoming work, nor one day's worth of outgoing work. Wouldn't it be nice just to have a list of tasks every day which covers all your outstanding work and which you can get through during the day? It sounds unlikely, perhaps, but I will be showing you how to achieve precisely that.

If for some reason they weren't able to get through a day's work in a day, they would be able to diagnose what the problem is and how to cure it

Life never works completely to plan and even if you have the best system in the world there will be times when you find that you are falling behind in your work. It is important to be able to tell why this is happening so that you can take action to put it right. You cannot afford the energy drain that comes from building up backlogs.

They would be able to achieve all their daily actions, such as email, paper, phone messages and one-off tasks, in super-quick time

However much you have your eye set on the big picture, you still have to deal with all the routine actions that make up the average day – that is unless you have other people to do them for you. What happens only too easily is that the pressure of keeping up with these relatively trivial actions stops you from dealing with the really meaningful things. You cannot, however, afford to neglect the 'trivial' things because if you do you will get more and more bogged down. What you need to be able to do is keep totally on top of them, so that they offer the minimum distraction. This involves being able to deal with them systematically and quickly. I will be showing you how to do this.

They would be able to get projects completed in the quickest possible time

There is a tendency for projects to get bogged down and move slowly so that they take much longer than is really necessary. Knowing how to get projects started and how to keep them moving is a major skill, which I will be teaching in this book. As a result you will be able to keep yourself right on target with your projects.

They would be able to identify exactly what the right workload is for them

I have already talked about limits in the first chapter. If you take on (or are given) too much work, what happens? The only thing that can happen is that some of it doesn't get done properly – or done at all. The trouble is that what gets done and what doesn't get done tends to happen more or less at random. Wouldn't it be better to take a conscious decision about what should and shouldn't be done? If you know what constitutes the right workload for you it is easier to make that sort of decision. I will be showing you how to identify exactly what is an appropriate personal workload for you.

They would be able to bring new work on-line without disrupting existing work

Very few people have any system for taking on new work. The result is that they have no way of handling the situation when they are given a new project. It has to be fitted into their existing work – but how? Because they have no way of telling what an appropriate workload would be for them, they are unlikely to turn the new project down because they feel they *should* be able to do it. As well as enabling you to identify the right workload for you, I will be showing you a simple system for bringing new work on-line.

They would know how to deal with genuine emergencies, without allowing themselves to be distracted by things that aren't genuine emergencies

Nothing is more disruptive than the randomising effect of interruptions and emergencies. But how many 'emergencies' are genuine emergencies? Yes, of course sometimes you have a fire alert or a child starts screaming, but most of our so-called 'emergencies' are nothing of the sort. If you have more than one genuine emergency a week then something is going badly wrong – unless of course you are a member of the emergency services. For office workers, most 'emergencies' are the result of not paying enough attention to a subject in the first place.

They would be able to get moving on all those things that they dream of doing 'some day'

Most of us have plenty of things that we would like to do some day. Some of them may have to wait until we have earned a lot of money or fulfilled some other condition.

But for many of these projects there is no reason why we can't do them now except for the fact that 'I just can't find the time' or 'I haven't been able get round to it'. I will be showing you a simple system that will allow you to get moving on these. Since they may well represent some of the most important things you will ever do, this is a skill worth having.

They would follow up properly

Many people have a tendency to work on one subject or project in a great burst of activity and then to forget about it. By the time they come back to it they have lost track of many of the threads. A project is like a house plant – it needs regular watering, otherwise it dies. So it is important to keep things moving. This means that systematic follow-up of projects is a must. I will be teaching you how to do this.

They would know how to keep control of tasks that they have delegated to other people

If you've ever found yourself using the expression 'It's quicker to do it yourself', you will know that delegation is fraught with difficulties. But keeping control of tasks you have delegated is easier than you think. I will be showing you the best methods of doing so.

They would be able to deal with other people's poor time management

Even when we've solved the problem of our own poor time management, we still have the problem of other people's poor time management to contend with. When we are working badly, we tend to react to things according

53

to how much noise (real or metaphorical) they are making at the time. It's important to remember that other people work in the same way, so if we want them to do our stuff for us, we need to make more noise than all the other things they have on their plates. And of course the best way to do that is by systematic follow-up.

They would be able to motivate themselves so that they can power through their day's work

What is the best way to motivate yourself for your daily work? Obviously, enjoying your work and having a clear vision are very important, but I don't believe that they are the most important things for keeping going during the daily grind. On the contrary, I believe that what gives us the most energy is the feeling of being totally on top of our work. If you are on top of something you have the energy to do it even if you don't particularly like the work.

Which would give you more motivation?

- Keeping your accounts up to date by entering the invoices, etc. every day so that your tax return is simply a matter of pressing a few buttons; or
- Saving everything up for a year and having a frantic end-of-year struggle to get your tax return submitted in time.

By the time you have finished reading this book you will know everything you need to keep on top of your work. The rest will be up to you!

Questionnaire

Tick the box if you feel that the statement usually applies to you.

❑ Do you complete your work every day?

❑ Do you know what a day's work consists of?

❑ If you find you are slipping, do you know how to diagnose what's wrong?

❑ Do you get through your daily routine, such as email, paper, phone messages and one-off tasks, as quickly as possible without being distracted?

❑ Do you get projects completed quickly and effectively?

❑ Do you know exactly what workload you are capable of handling?

❑ Do you know how to bring new work on-line without disrupting existing work?

❑ Can you distinguish genuine emergencies from mere distractions?

❑ Do you know what to do with all those things that you mean to get round to 'some day'?

❑ Do you follow up properly?

❑ Do you know how to keep tabs on tasks that you have delegated to other people?

❑ Can you overcome other people's poor time management?

❑ Do you keep motivated through the day's work?

❑ Do you know how to keep your projects on target?

4

The Problem with Time Management

Just because something would be nice to eat, doesn't mean you have to eat it.

In *Get Everything Done and Still Have Time to Play* I gave a list of things that I considered to be wrong with the standard methods of time management. I would like to concentrate on two of them here because they are fundamental to the way that I think we should be running our lives.

The two things I want to examine are the concept of prioritising by importance and the frequently used tool of making a to-do list. Both of these tend to be the sacred cows of time management, and I believe both of them are fundamentally wrong. The reason is the same in both cases: *they tend to make us do more of what gave us the problem in the first place.*

What gave us a time problem in the first place? Basically there are three possible causes, and *only* three possible causes. Of course the problem may be caused by all three at the same time. These causes are:

1 We are working inefficiently.
2 We have too much to do.
3 We have too little time to do it in.

Let's look at each of these in turn:

We are working inefficiently

Notice that I use the word 'inefficiently' rather than 'ineffectively'. This is deliberate, as here I am purely talking about how quickly we can process work. I am not in this context making any value judgment about whether we are doing the right work or not. It is our basic processing power that is in question.

If we are working in a distracted, unfocused, fragmented way we will not be processing work well. Most of us could probably increase our efficiency at processing work. If you pay attention to what this book says, you should make a major improvement. Yet however excellent our efficiency may become, we will nevertheless eventually come up against the physical limits of how much work one individual can do. Once we have reached those limits, we have to look elsewhere for a solution if we are still not on top of our work.

Beware – one problem that may occur if we become more efficient at processing work is that we are tempted to take on more work as a result. That can easily lead to our getting overwhelmed again – it will just be a bigger and better overwhelm!

We have too much to do

A very simple truth is that if we have more work than we are capable of processing then we won't be able to do it all properly. Unfortunately, like many simple truths, this tends to escape many people. I am frequently approached by potential clients who are already overloaded and want me to coach them so they can do even more. For many people being worked off their feet seems to be vital to their self-worth. Taking steps to cut their workload is tantamount to an admission of failure.

In fact the question is whether our capacity to process work is sufficient to deal with the workload that we have. As we've seen, we can increase our capacity up to certain limits; but once these limits have been exceeded the only thing we can do is to cut the work that we have.

It's no use just looking at individual items of work here. Work doesn't come from nowhere. It comes from the commitments that we have. Some of these may be ones we have been given and some may be ones we have taken on of our own accord, but however we came to take on our commitments they are the source of all the work that we have. To reduce our work, we need to reduce our commitments.

We have too little time to do it in

Whenever we look at an empty diary page in the future, we are deceiving ourselves if we think it is really empty. It is already full of all the stuff that we have to do every day. The temptation to schedule meetings, appointments, conferences, etc. as if an empty page meant that the day was absolutely empty must be resisted. You must leave adequate time to do your work – unless of course you have someone to do all your work for you.

If you think about it, you can see that these three reasons are the only possible ones for why you can't get through all your work. Every possible reason or excuse that we give for not getting everything done is contained under these three headings.

The trouble with the common time-management principle of prioritising by importance is that it encourages us to make each of these three causes worse.

- *We are working inefficiently* If we are working inefficiently, prioritising by importance is not going to help us because it does not make any difference to the rate at which we are processing work. We may be doing so-called 'important' stuff badly or so-called 'unimport-ant' stuff badly, but we are still doing it badly. Putting our work into a different order doesn't increase the speed or efficiency with which we are working. Instead it can lead to our having multiple backlogs of 'unimport-ant' stuff. Once these get too big, even the 'important' stuff will be too clogged up to get actioned. Prioritising by importance encourages us to think that it makes us work more efficiently, when the reverse is the case.

- *We have too much to do* If we have too much work, prioritising by importance won't help to cut down the amount of work we have. It won't increase the amount of work we get through either. Inevitably some work is not going to get done. If it's so unimportant that we can afford for it not to be done, then why are we trying to do it in the first place? If it does need to be done, then does it really make any difference what order we do it in? The truth is that once we have taken on commitments, we need to do everything that relates to them. Prioritising by importance is a means of avoiding the real question – which is: should I be doing this in the first place? By giving us the illusion that we can prioritise ourselves out of trouble by concentrating on the 'important' stuff, it positively encourages us to take too much on.

• *We have too little time to do it in* If we are overscheduled and are not leaving enough time, then prioritising by importance does nothing to help us. By again giving us the illusion that we can prioritise ourselves out of trouble, it positively encourages us to overschedule.

To-do lists do nothing to help us either. All a to-do list consists of is a more or less complete list of outstanding tasks which has no relation to a day's work. If you think about it, you need to be able to get through one day's incoming work in one day on average. In an ideal world you would deal with all the incoming work every day and would complete everything you have to do every day. To most people this sounds totally impossible, but it is in fact quite achievable. The reason it sounds impossible is that to-do lists have destroyed the connection between the work that comes in during a day and the work that we do during a day.

Test yourself

Which is the best answer (A or B) in each of these scenarios?

1 You are setting up your own small business. Someone mentions a new opportunity to you which would complement your business nicely. Do you:

A Take on the new opportunity, and integrate the new work with your present work?

B Decide that the last thing you need is a
distraction from setting up your business,
however tempting the opportunity seems?

2 Your day seems to be full of distractions and you
spend your time so buried in trivial stuff that you can
never get around to the important stuff. Do you:

A Decide to prioritise your day better so that the
important stuff gets done before the trivial stuff?

B Work out better systems for dealing with routine
matters?

3 Your job entails a lot of travelling and meetings. Your
meetings generate quite a bit of administrative work,
but your schedule is so full that you find yourself
getting way behind on dealing with the administration.
Do you:

A Find someone else to deal with the administrative
work (possibly by hiring them)?

B Schedule in a minimum amount of time each
week to deal with the administrative work?

Answers:

1 B is correct. Think of opportunities as items on a menu
in a restaurant. Just because something would be nice
to eat, doesn't mean you have to eat it. To take on a
new commitment when you are in the middle of
setting up a business is the best way to sabotage your
business.

2 B is correct. This is a case of working inefficiently. You
need to improve your systems so the trivial stuff gets
actioned efficiently and is kept firmly in its place. If
you try to prioritise by doing the 'important' stuff first,

the 'trivial' stuff will not get done. You will soon discover that it will assert its importance in some very unpleasant ways.

3 Both answers are correct, and the best solution would probably be a combination of both. However, note that if A is impossible for some reason then B is the only remaining solution. Carrying on the way you are is not an option.

Exercise

Make a complete list of all the tasks that you have outstanding at the moment. Now write down beside each item approximately how long that task has been outstanding for. In other words, how long ago was it that you were given the task, took it on or decided that it needed doing?

What you will probably discover is that the items on the list have come in over quite a long period of time. Some may have come in today or yesterday. Some may be a week or so old. A few may be months or even years old.

Next, ask yourself how many days' work your to-do list would take to clear if you did nothing but work on it until every item on the list was crossed off. The easiest way to do this is to make a time estimate in minutes for each item on the list, add them all together, divide by sixty to give you the number of hours, and then divide again by the number of hours you work a day to tell you how many days' worth of work you have.

Even working in ideal circumstances, it would probably take quite a few days before you succeeded in clearing the list. So what you can see quite clearly is that this list of things you have to do neither represents a day's worth of incoming work, nor does it represent a day's worth of outgoing work. This is common to all to-do lists.

Now do the next exercise, which will show you what a day's worth of work really looks like.

Exercise

What I want you to do here is to collect a day's worth of incoming work. I'm asking you to write down during the course of one working day every single item of work that comes in during the day, regardless of whether you action it or not. Record how many emails you receive and how many phone calls or other messages. Itemise the pieces of paper that come in. Write down all tasks that fall due or which you are given that day.

Don't include anything that is already on your to-do list or any backlogs of work. That's all old work!

At the end of the day, look at the list. That is one day's worth of incoming work. Have a good look at it. That is the amount of work you have to get through every day on average if you are to stay completely on top. Can you do it?

If you know that this was an exceptionally heavy or exceptionally light day for incoming work, you can make a mental adjustment. But basically this is it – this is what you need to do on average every working day. Is it doable?

Some people may be pleasantly surprised when they do this exercise. They realise that if they could get away from the clogging effect of old undone work, they would in fact be able to keep up quite easily.

Some people may be horrified. If that's what they are

trying to get through every day, no wonder they can't keep up!

Either way, maybe for the first time ever, you have a clear picture of how much work is meant by 'a day's work'.

Standard methods of time management give you no guidance about what a day's work should consist of. All they offer is a means of manipulating the order in which you do your work in an attempt to avoid the consequences of not balancing your incoming work with your outgoing work. Manipulating your work by trying to do the 'important' things first is never going to be more than a sticking-plaster approach to the problem. The real causes lie at a deeper level and must be addressed.

You have seen what one day's worth of work consists of. You now need to take on board the fact that this is the average amount of work that you have to be able to clear every day. If you are not able to clear it, then the only remedies are to:

- Increase your efficiency at processing work.
- Reduce the amount of work that you have.
- Increase the amount of time available for work.

There are no other ways around the problem. When you find yourself falling behind on your work, one or more of these *must* be the answer. For most people it's probably a combination of these factors that is at fault. They are distracted and unfocused because they have allowed their commitments to grow unchecked and undefined. This makes work unpleasant and stressful so they over-schedule themselves because meetings are a way of avoiding work and make a good excuse for being behind. It is very difficult to break out of this sort of vicious circle once it has become established.

I want to make it clear here that I am only unhappy about the concept of prioritising one's *tasks* by importance. Prioritising tasks is to be prioritising at the wrong level. The right place for prioritising is at the level of goals and commitments. Since all your work flows from your commitments, it is absolutely essential to be selective about which commitments you are going to take on. The only sensible way of doing this is to decide which are the really important ones for your life and work.

Once you have made a commitment, all the work relevant to it needs to be done. Questions of importance and non-importance become irrelevant. Many people spend their lives 'fire-fighting' because they have neglected this basic point. It is very important to realise that work does not appear out of thin air. It appears as a result of commitments that you have made. Every commitment results in work, and every bit of work that you have results from some commitment, whether you have made that commitment consciously or not.

Most commitments are themselves the result of a higher commitment. So you have a chain of commitments. Some commitments are made to yourself, some to members of your family, some to your work, some to your friends and colleagues, some to organisations of one kind or another that you belong to.

When you are trying to cut down your workload, the place to look is not at your individual tasks, but at your commitments. When we feel the need to cut our workload, there is a marked tendency to do it by cutting the time we allocate to each commitment, rather than by cutting the commitments themselves. It is much more sensible to cut our commitments so we have adequate time to complete them all. Commitments are like bushes – they need regular pruning.

Exercise:

Look at each item on your to-do list and ask yourself why you have put that item on the list. What commitment have you made that involves doing it? Is it really a valid commitment that it is reasonable to have at the moment? Even if all your commitments are valid, is it reasonable to have them *all* at the same time?

In the next chapter we will be looking at the sort of things we should be taking into account when we decide what our commitments should be.

5

Real Work v. Busy Work

Busy work often looks more like work than real work does.

As I have been emphasising in the last chapter, trying to prioritise by importance is essentially saying, 'What am I going to do well and what am I going to do badly?' The real question is, 'Should I be doing this at all?'

You will have gathered by now that I strongly believe that when you take on a commitment you need to do it properly. Taking things on that you are not going to do properly is pointless, and only ensures that your chances of doing other things properly are diminished as well. If you are not going to do something properly, you would be better off making a conscious choice not to do it at all. It is better to do a few things well than a lot of things badly. How should we decide what those few things are that we are going to do well?

Whenever you take on a new commitment you must carefully consider what the effect is going to be on your existing commitments. Strangely enough we are all already filling twenty-four hours each day with *something*. Whenever we take on *something new, something else* is going to have to give up some of the time that we are currently spending on it. That's fine if the *something else* consists of sitting around aimlessly watching television. It's also fine if time is being released by another project that is coming to an end. It's not so fine if we are already having trouble fitting everything in.

I have already talked about the fact that goals are as much about what we are *not* going to do as they are about what we are going to do. Exactly the same is true about our commitments. They don't just spell out what we are committed to. They also imply that we are *not going to get involved with anything else* that would take us away from that commitment. That's what commitment means. In marriage for example we can see only too clearly what happens if one of the partners fails to make that commitment properly.

So whenever you draw up a list of your commitments, it is essentially saying, 'This is what I am going to confine myself to.' Out of the fog of differing demands on your time, ideas, suggestions, whims, etc., your commitments should stand out like a lighthouse from the angry sea: 'These are what I am going to confine myself to.'

It's easy to get immersed in lots of activity, without really taking much action. In the field of government we often see a lot of activity and not much action. Politicians are often criticised for thinking that talking about a problem or passing a law about a problem is the same as solving the problem.

Exactly the same applies in most fields of endeavour. Activity is not the same as action – though it is often mistaken for it. It's easy to fool oneself that being frantically busy is the same thing as doing real work.

So I want to draw a distinction here between 'real work' and 'busy work'. This is a very fundamental distinction, especially if you are in a situation where it is you who make the running.

Real work is what advances your business or your job. It should use your skills and knowledge to the full and will frequently take you out of your comfort zone. Since it is by nature quite challenging, it is likely to meet some resistance within your mind.

Busy work, on the other hand, is what you do in order to avoid doing the real work!

Real work often involves a lot of thinking and planning. The unfortunate result of this is that busy work often looks more like work than real work does. If you are rushing around looking busy, it gives the appearance that you are working far more than if you are sitting quietly thinking and planning. It looks like that to your colleagues – and worst of all it often looks like that to you.

I've lost count of the number of times I've heard people say, 'I really must do such-and-such, but I simply can't find the time.' Very often the such-and-such that they haven't got around to doing is something absolutely crucial to their business, such as designing a marketing plan or revamping their website. Why can't they find the time to do what may well be the most important thing they could do? Because they are bogged down in minor commitments which they have taken on and now feel obliged to fulfil. Essentially these commitments are busy work that there was no real need to take on in the first place.

Exactly what busy work consists of will vary from person to person and job to job. One person's real work is another person's busy work. So, for example, if a boss spends her time doing work that her assistant could handle, it is busy work for her even though it is her assistant's real work.

Real work	Busy work
Advances your business or job	Avoids the work necessary for advancing your business or job
Consists of what you are paid for or what makes you money	Gets in the way of what you are paid for or what makes you money
Impacts the bottom line positively	Has a negative effect on the bottom line
Uses your skills and knowledge to the full	Underuses your skills and knowledge
Takes you out of your comfort zone	Keeps you within your comfort zone
Challenging	Easy
Only you can do it	Anyone can do it

Here are a few pointers to help you identify whether you are doing real work or busy work. You have probably fallen into the busy work trap:

- *If your work overwhelms you but doesn't challenge you* Real work is challenging but not overwhelming.
- *If a lot of the work you are doing is the same as the work that people under you are doing* Real work requires your individual skills and experience. If what you are doing could be done by someone who doesn't have that skill and experience, you are working below your capacity.
- *If there are some vital actions that you haven't got around to* Real work *is* those vital actions.
- *If you never have time to stop and think* Real work is thought expressing itself in action. If you are not thinking, you are unlikely to be doing any real work.

- *If your time horizon is always very short* Real work involves planning further ahead than the immediate horizon.
- *If you are continually bumping up against the same problems* Real work insists on excellent systems to support it.

It's immensely important to identify what the real work is in your job. Perhaps I should rather say 'in your life', because the concept of real work applies to your personal life as well. What actions are really going to take your life forward?

A good rule to use here is: 'Never say yes to anything unless you can say it whole-heartedly.' When someone asks you to take on a new commitment, the tendency is either to accept grudgingly or to refuse and feel guilty about it. Instead, get into the habit of asking yourself the question: 'Can I say a whole-hearted yes to this?' If the answer is 'yes', you can accept in the knowledge that you can make a whole-hearted commitment to it. If the answer is 'no' then you can decline by saying, 'I have a rule that I never take anything on unless I can make a whole-hearted commitment to it, and I don't believe I can in this case.'

This is extremely important, because if you take something on without making a whole-hearted commitment to it you will inevitably end up doing it less than well, and probably resenting it into the bargain. Our language bears witness to this: 'He doesn't have his heart in it'; 'She did it half-heartedly'; 'I don't have the heart for it'; 'At heart they don't really support this.'

71

Test yourself

What would be your real work in the following situations?

1 You are the owner of a small business.
2 You are a salesperson for a small educational products firm.
3 You are personal assistant to the managing director of a large company.
4 You are a life coach working on your own.

Answers

1 The most important part of your real work as a business owner is what only you can do, i.e. provide strategy and direction for the business. Too many business owners get so immersed in the business itself that they lose sight of the essentials.
2 It's tempting to say that your real work is selling things. In fact your real work is the actions that will lead to your selling things. You need to identify what these actions are. In most cases it boils down to making lots of calls. If you are not making lots of calls, you are not doing your real work.
3 Your real work is to free up the managing director so she can do her real work.
4 In this sort of situation it's important to identify what sort of business you are in. Your profession is coaching, but your business is selling coaching services. If you are not spending lots of time on selling and marketing, you are not doing real work.

Earlier on in this book I said that what motivates us best for our day's work is to be completely on top of it. You might not have been expecting that answer. Most people would probably say, 'Clear goals', 'Enthusiasm', 'Work I love doing' or something else on those lines. You may have been surprised that I didn't think it was any of those things.

If we are totally on top of our work we have the energy for it, even if it isn't work we particularly enjoy.

To be on top of our work we must have clear goals that define both what we are going to do and what we are not going to do. Enthusiasm will come from the knowledge that our goals are real goals about real work – work that is going to use all our skills and talents in the business of taking our lives forwards. We love our work when our work is under our control – but not when we are under its control.

I have mentioned earlier the metaphor of ordering from a restaurant menu. When we order a meal, we are in effect saying that we are not going to eat any of the other possible meals – however delicious they may sound. This leads to a very important principle. Just because something sounds like a great opportunity or sounds like something you would really like to do, doesn't mean that you have to do it!

People who are into network marketing often seem to suffer from the disease of looking for the next great opportunity. Whatever your opinion of network market-ing, its structure means that a few people make a lot of money, some people make a small amount of money, and the vast majority lose money.

The difference between the people who make money at

network marketing and the people who don't can generally be summed up in one word: persistence. The people who make money choose one firm and stick to it. They will keep working at it steadily for a long period of time. The people who lose money at network marketing are usually tempted by the promise of instant riches and when these don't materialise they give up, or go off to another 'better' opportunity. I have come across people who have tried dozens of network marketing opportunities and never made any money at any of them. Rather than constantly trying to find the 'perfect' opportunity, they would have done much better to pick almost any one opportunity and stick to it. Even if they picked a bad one and it went bust, they would have learned an immense amount from the experience of sticking to it.

This failing isn't exclusive to people in network marketing. The same is true for many people in business in general. They come across a good idea or a new opportunity and launch into it. They remain blissfully unaware of the fact that the main effect of the new opportunity is to dilute the effort they are putting into their existing business.

The way to make money in business is usually to keep your focus as narrow as possible. Your aim should be to do a few things really well. If you find you don't have time to do them all really well, then narrow your focus even further so that you are doing even fewer things!

It sounds easy enough to narrow your focus when you are self-employed or the boss of your own small business, but how do you narrow your focus when you have a boss, and it's he or she who is dishing out the projects and commitments?

Employees need to resist the temptation to sit back and blame all their time-management problems on their boss. Your boss has the responsibility of seeing that you are well managed and properly tasked, and it is your responsibility to provide him or her with the information and feedback to do that well.

If you are going to approach your boss about your workload, it is important to have a clear idea yourself of the way your job should be carried out. If you don't have that clarity yourself, then how are you going to put your recommendations over to your boss? To fight your corner you must be clear what your corner consists of.

6
Emergency, What Emergency?

A pseudo-emergency is one that is an emergency only because you have not done it earlier.

Imagine that you get your car serviced at Joe Slobb's Auto Repairs. Joe is a great mechanic and can do wonderful things with cars, but he's a one-man band and completely disorganised. When anyone calls him wanting to book their car in for a service or repair, Joe will tell them to 'bring it in whenever you like'. At any one time he has about ten cars littered around his repair shop in various states of dismantlement. He does a bit of work on one and then gets tired of it and moves on to another. Then someone rings him up to tell him they need their car urgently so he moves over to work on their car – until the next phone interruption, that is.

Joe's working day is constantly interspersed with the demands of irate customers who want to know where their cars are. They quickly get to know that even if their car requires only a couple of hours' work they need to budget for it being out of action for at least a week, possibly longer.

The advantage of being able to get their car into the workshop whenever they like doesn't seem quite such an advantage when they can't get it back again. In fact, quite often the only reason some of his customers don't go in to forcibly reclaim their cars is because they know they will be in pieces. Even when they do finally get their cars back, they will often find that Joe has forgotten all about some important bit of work.

Joe just about gets away with it because he can do miracles with almost any type of car and he is very cheap.

Now does the way that Joe organises, or rather fails to organise, his work ring any bells? Truth to tell it resembles very closely the way an awful lot of people spend their days – whether they are in a repair shop, in an office or even at home.

Joe has a rival mechanic in town, called Mick Cool. Mick is no better mechanic than Joe, but he does have one great advantage – he is very well organised. When someone calls to get his or her car repaired, Mick will book the car in for a specific day. He knows exactly how many days ahead he is committed already, and he knows from experience pretty well how long any given repair is likely to take. That means he knows how many cars he can book in on any given day. When a customer books a car in for a certain day, he knows he is going to get it back on the same day.

Mick makes a checklist of the work that needs to be done on each car, so he never forgets to do anything. He works on one car at a time, completes the checklist and moves on to the next car. If he comes across an unexpected problem he will deal with it there and then if he can. If he can't, he will call the customer to book it in again for another day. Unlike Joe, Mick goes home at the same time each day, confident that he has done all the work he had to do that day. His reliability means that he can charge much more than Joe does. And who do you think repairs the larger number of cars during the week?

Ask yourself whenever you feel pressured: am I being Joe Slobb or Mick Cool?

Joe is the living embodiment of all that can go wrong with time management. Let's look in detail at the way he works and see how much of it applies to us as well.

- He has not established limits for his work.
- He reacts to whatever catches his attention.
- He is working on a large number of things at the same time.
- He has no real idea of how much work he can do in a day.
- He does not complete his work every day.

Result: in the attempt to please everyone all of the time, Joe is inefficient, has less capacity than Mick, lets people down, and has to work for less than his skills should be worth.

Mick on the other hand works in a quite different way.

- He has established limits for his work.
- He does not allow himself to be distracted.
- He works on one thing at a time.
- He knows exactly how much work he can do in a day.
- He completes his work every day.

Result: although people have to wait longer initially, they will get their cars back more quickly and with everything done properly. He is efficient, has a high capacity, does not let people down, and can charge what his skills are worth.

Joe Slobb	Mick Cool
Has not established limits	Has established limits
Reacts to whatever catches his attention	Does not allow himself to be distracted
Works on a large number of things at the same time	Works on one thing at a time
Has no real idea of how much work he can do in a day	Knows exactly how much work he can do in a day
Does not complete his work every day	Completes his work every day
Low capacity	High capacity
Long turn around time	Short turn around time

What is the essential difference between Joe's way of working and Mick's? It can be summed up in one word: *random*.

Joe's day is almost entirely random. It is random how many cars come into his workshop any given day; it is random what he does to them, and it is random when the owners get them back.

Presented with exactly the same circumstances of random bookings by customers, Mick immediately imposes order on them. His work is almost entirely non-random. Even when the unexpected occurs, Mick quickly moves to impose order on it.

Now how does Mick impose order on the random sequence of car bookings? He does it by creating some distance between himself and the booking. He has a buffer zone in which the random bookings can accumulate and be put into order. Joe on the other hand creates no distance between himself and whatever chances to happen. He just reacts to whatever presents itself.

Notice that Mick does not just create distance; he also imposes an ordered sequence. Creating distance without imposing an ordered sequence is known as 'putting it off' and simply means that you have stored up a random impulse for the future.

This method of creating distance and imposing an ordered sequence is at the heart of good time management.

Exercise

Observe yourself during the course of a working day. Look out for the occasions when you are tempted to do something random. This may be in response to a sudden impulse. Or it may be the result of a request by someone else, or something unexpected occurring. Make a note of the times you are tempted, whether you actually do the random action or not.

Typical examples of random actions:

- Every time your computer tells you a new email has arrived, you leave what you are doing in order to read it.
- You do loads of minor tasks rather than get on with the important project you promised yourself you would work on.
- A client rings up with a request and you drop everything in order to attend it.
- You get a bright idea and start investigating it immediately.
- Your boss dumps some work on your desk and you abandon all your plans for the day.
- Someone recommends a website to you and you

immediately go off and spend forty minutes looking at it.

• You remember something you've forgotten to do and rush off to action it.

These are only a few examples out of an endless universe of possibilities!

The common factor with all of these is that you acted immediately in response to a random stimulus without first creating distance and then imposing order on it. In other words, you have no buffer zone.

The creation of a buffer zone depends on being very clear about what degree of urgency something merits. Be warned that this is a subject where there is huge scope for self-deception. Frequently, people also have a great deal of resistance to analysing the different degrees of urgency that they should be giving to their work. So I am asking you to read the following with an open mind. If you find yourself resisting some of it, be prepared to challenge yourself about your preconceptions.

For the purposes of time management I distinguish three degrees of urgency:

• Immediate;
• Same day;
• Tomorrow.

Note that these do not in any way refer to the importance of the tasks. They refer only to the size of the buffer that you put into place. The ideal is to collect all actions and deal with them tomorrow. This gives you the ability to plan your day fully without losing the ability to make a quick response. However, some items require a faster response, and these will fall into the 'Immediate' or 'Same day' categories. Let's look at each of these in turn.

Immediate

The 'immediate' degree of urgency relates only to things that require you to drop everything else and give your immediate attention to them. Some people's jobs consist of immediate actions like this. If you are a member of the emergency services such as a fire officer or a paramedic, a large part of your work consists of responding immediately to emergencies. If you are a shop assistant or a cashier in a bank or post office your work also consists of providing immediate services.

What is important to note about all these jobs is that they are organised to provide an immediate response. Although the emergencies or the customers are random, the response that is made to them is not at all random. The way the job is organised imposes order on the situation. With the emergency services there are communications and procedures, together with the appropriate trained personnel with their equipment. In the case of shops, banks and similar organisations there are also procedures and trained staff.

In these organisations, if something goes wrong with the provision of immediate responses, it is not a time-management problem – it is an organisational problem. If the ambulance takes two hours to arrive at an accident, it's because the ambulances are badly organised, or there are not enough of them or they are understaffed, or possibly that the staff are badly trained. These are all organisational matters, not time-management matters. If the queue at the post office stretches 200 yards down the street, it's because there aren't enough counters or enough staff or the staff aren't properly trained, or because procedures are too cumbersome. All these are organisational problems, not time-management problems.

Now how much of your work requires an immediate response? Be very honest with yourself here. How much of it *requires* an immediate response? How much of it requires an *immediate* response? Remember that an immediate response implies that you will drop everything else to give that response.

Test yourself

Which of these merits an immediate response?

1   Your telephone rings.
2   You answer the phone and it is a client asking a simple question, which you know the answer to.
3   You answer the phone and it is a client asking a question that you will have to research.
4   Smoke starts drifting past your window and the fire alarm goes off.
5   Your computer pings and the 'You have mail' box appears.
6   Your boss dumps a load of work on your desk and says she needs it by close of play today.
7   Someone tells you the office photocopier isn't working. You are the only one who knows how to fix it.
8   Your computer won't start.

9 You suddenly remember you have forgotten your best friend's birthday.

10 Your boss sends you an email saying, 'Let me know what you think about this. I've got a meeting about it this afternoon.'

11 A colleague drops by your desk to tell you about his holiday.

12 A colleague drops by your desk to tell you about the latest progress on an important work project.

13 You are pushed for time to get ready for an important presentation in the afternoon. Suddenly a client rings up with a major crisis, which you are going to have to resolve this morning.

14 A member of the public rings you up asking for details of your product.

Answers

1 *Answering* the telephone is an immediate task – unless you have decided that you are not going to answer the telephone at all because you are working on something that needs concentrated attention. It's your decision. If excessive telephone calls are a problem, this will be an organisational matter which needs to be addressed.

2 The degree of urgency relates to the *content* of the question rather than whether you can answer it or not. However, this is a case where if you know the answer off the top of your head it is quicker and easier to get it out of the way immediately.

3 This is not immediate – unless the caller is asking for first-aid advice from the scene of an accident.

It's the *content* of the phone call that the degree of urgency relates to, not the fact that it's a phone call.

4 This is a genuine emergency. An immediate reaction is called for!

5 This is absolutely not something that requires immediate action. In fact I recommend turning off the new-mail notification altogether.

6 This justifies a *quick* response, but not an *immediate* one.

7 This probably deserves an immediate response, even though it is at the cost of interrupting your work. The fact that you are being interrupted by this type of query is an organisational problem and you need to ask organisational questions, such as 'Why am I the only person who knows how to fix the photocopier?'

8 This definitely requires an immediate response, since the whole of the rest of your work depends on it.

9 This may merit a quick response, but not an immediate one. After all, why did you forget the birthday in the first place? Because you don't work systematically and in an ordered fashion, that's why!

10 This needs a quick response but not an immediate one.

11 Generally speaking it's OK to give an immediate response to this type of interruption, assuming it will take only a couple of minutes. However, if interruptions like this are a problem for you, then remember the answer will be an organisational one, not a time-management one.

12 If this is going to take more than a few minutes it's

best to arrange a time when you can discuss it
properly.

13 An immediate response is required but *not* to the
crisis itself! Your immediate response should be to
take a moment or two to work out the implications,
and if necessary arrange for someone else to do
some of the preparatory work for the presentation.
This will allow you to respond to the crisis in an
ordered and rational way.

14 Give them an immediate response. However, if you
have a large number of such calls coming in it is
important to spend time considering how best to
organise the response to them.

Same day

One of the most difficult things to establish in our minds
is the difference between something that requires an
immediate response and something that requires a quick,
same-day response. It sounds like a trivial difference, but
there is all the difference in the world between them from
a time-management point of view.

For my purposes I define a 'same-day' response as a
response that isn't immediate but needs to take place
sometime within the same day. This is a purely utilitarian
definition. The key point is that if you need to make a
response the same day, you can't plan for it when you are
making out your plan for the day. Items requiring a quick
response are therefore extremely difficult to handle.

In fact, 'same-day' items are more difficult to handle than
'immediate' items from a time-management perspective.
This is because, as we saw above, responses to

'immediate' items are a matter of organisation, not time management. In the case of unexpected emergencies, the response is obvious: you don't need to sit around prioritising while the building is burning down – you just get out of the building.

The above of course assumes that you are making the right distinction between 'immediate' and 'same-day'. One of the major reasons for fractured, unfocused work is the failure to make this distinction. Many people have a tendency to react to everything immediately, whether it really merits it or not. This means that whatever they were working on at the time gets abandoned while the new thing is taken up. This in turn gets abandoned when something else catches their attention. They are in other words being exactly like Joe Slobb.

We have to train ourselves to put distance between ourselves and the thing that needs a quick response. We need a buffer so that we can impose some order. In the answer to question 13 in the last exercise, I showed one way of creating a buffer when a crisis arose that needed a very quick response – but not an immediate response. Note that if the person had reacted to the crisis by leaping into immediate action, they would probably have gone rushing around in a state of high stress and panic. Instead their immediate response to the crisis was to create a buffer by writing down everything that they needed to do. It was then possible to deal with the crisis in an ordered way instead of in a purely reactive way.

This is necessary because different parts of the brain take the leading role when we are being reactive and when we are being ordered. When we are being reactive, primitive parts of the brain such as the brain stem are taking the lead. When we are being ordered, the more evolved rational parts of the brain such as the neo-cortex are dominant.

The reactive brain is very useful when we are faced with a genuine emergency – but it positively gets in the way when we are trying to make a rational plan of action. When we create a buffer we are switching our brain over from reactive to rational thinking.

One of the best ways of achieving this is to write down what we intend to do. Being a higher-level activity, writing automatically switches us into a more rational mode. You can experience this for yourself. Watch your mind and wait for an impulse to arrive in your mind. It could be something like 'I need a cup of coffee' or 'That link looks interesting'. Then, instead of going and getting a cup of coffee or clicking on the link, write down 'Get cup of coffee' or 'Investigate www.markforster.net'. Observe what happens when you do this. If you then get the coffee or investigate the link, you are no longer doing it out of impulse but as a more rational considered decision. More likely you will decide that it's not worth interrupting your current work for, so you will defer it.

You need to make a rule for yourself here: whenever something comes up that you think needs a quick response, write it down. It's good to keep a separate list for doing this. The act of writing it down will help you to decide whether the item really does require a quick response within the same day or whether it can be left until tomorrow without damage. Making a habit of this is crucial because when you are designing your day you cannot plan for same-day actions. This means that you must keep same-day items to the absolute minimum consistent with the aims of your work. If you fail to do this, your day will be filled with random factors – and remember: random factors are the most disruptive influence on your work.

I will be saying more later about the best way to write these items down to gain the maximum effect.

Test yourself

Which of these situations merits a same-day response?

1   You haven't yet started on a report which is due in by the end of the day. You've had a week to do it, but you haven't been able to get around to it before.

2   A client calls you and asks you to send him some information. You have it all in a file, so all you have to do is email it to him.

3   A client calls you and asks you to send her some information. You are going to have to research it.

4   Your boss dumps a load of work on your desk and says he needs it by the end of the day.

5   Your boss dumps a load of work on your desk and says she needs it by the end of the week (today is Tuesday).

6   Your computer has developed an annoying fault. It doesn't stop you from working but it really bugs you.

7   A friend sends you an email which says, 'You really must look at this website. It's right up your street.'

8   A colleague sends you an email which says, 'You really must look at this website. It's got a lot of the information we need for Project X.'

9   A colleague emails you with a non-urgent question
     that only needs a one-word reply.
10   Someone brings in a load of information which you
     have been waiting for in order to complete an
     important report.

Answers

1   Since it's due in by the end of the day you'd better
     do it, hadn't you? But why did you get yourself in
     this situation in the first place? This is an example of
     a pseudo-emergency, i.e. one that is an emergency
     only because you have not done it earlier. These
     false emergencies are very destructive to your time
     and you need to avoid them at all costs. Fortunately
     the rest of this book will tell you how!

2   Since there's no indication that the request is urgent,
     it does not merit a same-day response. Remember
     the degree of urgency relates to the *content* of the
     request, not to the fact that it is a phone call.

3   Same answer as question 2. However, please note
     that if either of the requests had been urgent they
     would have merited a same-day response, regardless
     of whether you just had to send a file or had to
     research the information. The degree of urgency
     relates to the *content* of the request, not to how
     easy it is to fulfil it.

4   If you want to keep your job, this had better be
     dealt with the same day. However, if you are
     pushed to complete the work you already have, you
     might want to check out with your boss whether all
     the new work is urgent or just some of it.

5 Definitely does not require a same-day response.

6 Since it's not preventing you from working, it does not merit a same-day response. Although there may be a slight advantage in doing it today, the benefit does not outweigh the disruption caused by introducing a random factor into your day – especially as anything to do with computer faults can be guaranteed to take ten times longer than you expected.

7 It'll still be right up your street tomorrow, so it doesn't need looking at today!

8 There's no indication that Project X is urgent, so this does not merit same-day action.

9 Remember the degree of urgency of the response depends on the urgency of the request, not on how easy it is to respond. I would be fooling you if I said that I would never reply to an email like this the same day. But if I do I usually end up regretting it, because once I start responding to one email I tend to go on and respond to others. Also I find that a too rapid reply to an email can lead to emails batting back and forth all day. My advice is not to answer it today unless your colleague says it's urgent.

10 The question says the report is important, but there is no indication that it is urgent. This does not merit a same-day response, though you may be very tempted to give it one. Resist the temptation – a random factor is a random factor even if it's an important one!

Tomorrow

Ideally, all your work should be fitted into this category. Why is that so important? The reason is that these items can be planned. When you make your plan for the day, these are the ones that you know about. One of the great secrets of time management is not to give things more urgency than they deserve. Never react to anything immediately unless it is a genuine emergency or your job is to provide immediate responses and you are organised to do so. Never do anything the same day unless there is a significant downside to not doing it the following day. It needs to be a *significant* downside because the benefits of not doing things the same day in general far outweigh any minor advantage that is gained by a quick reaction.

Your 'default setting' should be '*Do it tomorrow*'. You should be prepared to change it only when there is a very good reason. If you are in doubt, then it can wait till tomorrow!

Remember that whenever you give something the degree of urgency of 'immediate' or 'same-day', it becomes a random factor in your day. If you give something the degree of urgency of 'tomorrow' it can be planned – that means it is no longer random. I want to stress again how important it is that you classify as much of your work as possible in this category.

Test yourself

Which of these should be classified as 'Tomorrow'?

1   You get a bright idea while travelling to work, which

you want to think about further. You don't want to lose the idea.

2   You go to a meeting and come back with a load of points in your briefcase for action.

3   Bill Gates calls you personally and says that he is considering bundling your product with every copy of Windows. He wants to know how quickly you can get a proposal to him.

4   You notice that the clock on your computer has been set to the wrong time zone.

5   You can't quite make up your mind whether something needs to be done today or whether you could leave it to tomorrow.

6   There is a message on your voicemail from a client, asking you to call her back.

7   You notice that the drawer in your desk is getting untidy.

8   You receive 106 emails during the course of the day.

9   A colleague asks you urgently for some figures for a report because he's 'got to get it in today'.

10   A client asks you to send him some figures.

Answers

1   Note it down for investigation tomorrow.

2   Empty the contents of your briefcase into your in-tray for action tomorrow.

3   This is the opportunity you have been waiting for your whole life. You don't need to plan or prioritise it – you just need to get moving. You want to be on the next available plane to his headquarters with a complete presentation.

4   Make a note to fix it tomorrow.

5   'Do it tomorrow' is your default setting. You only
    change it when there is a very good reason. If you
    are in doubt, 'Do it tomorrow'.

6   Unless the client has indicated that it's urgent, make
    a note to ring her tomorrow.

7   Careful! This is exactly the sort of thing that makes a
    fine displacement activity if you are resisting a major
    task. The correct response is to make a note to tidy
    it tomorrow.

8   That number of emails can keep you answering
    email all day if you are not careful. Keep an eye on
    the incoming email to see if there is anything
    genuinely urgent. Keep the rest for tomorrow and
    deal with them in one batch. This is by far the
    fastest way of dealing with email.

9   'I've got to get it in today' is usually code for 'I've
    left it till the last minute'. There's no reason why his
    inefficiency should ruin your day, so tell him that
    you can't get him the figures until tomorrow.

10 Tell him, 'I'll get them to you tomorrow without fail.'

Let's have a look at what happens if we get these degrees
of urgency wrong.

Generally speaking there are two main errors that people
fall into with degrees of urgency. The first is to classify too
many items as immediate. The second is to defer action on
items until a mythical time in the future called 'later'. In
fact for many people these are the only two classifications
that they are in practice using – 'immediate' or 'later'. The
problem with this is that they know from experience that
if they defer something until 'later' it has a tendency to get

postponed indefinitely. To compensate, they therefore tend to classify far too much as immediate, as that's the only way they can be sure of getting it done. This has the unfortunate effect of ruining any chance of dealing with things in an ordered and methodical way so that *everything* does in fact get done.

It is a serious problem when too many items get classed as immediate. When people are trying to deal with things on an immediate basis the effect is to send them jumping around, reacting to every stimulus. This produces the familiar fractured feeling that makes so many people's working days so stressful. Joe Slobb is a good example of someone who is wrongly giving everything the immediate degree of urgency. Because he wants to please everyone by being seen to take immediate action on their requests, he ends up giving a poorer service than Mick Cool, who makes no pretence of taking immediate action.

The immediate degree of urgency must be restricted to emergency services and to such situations as face-to-face interaction with customers, helplines, order lines and similar. Other than those, only genuine unexpected emergencies should qualify. Generally speaking, immediate items should not represent a time-management problem. If they are causing a problem, it will usually be an organisational problem or a health and safety one.

'Same-day' items present a considerable time-management problem. They are relatively frequent, and introduce disruptive random elements into the day because they can't be predicted (if it were possible to predict them, they would not be 'same-day' items as they could be planned for). As I keep saying, it is extremely important to keep these items to the absolute minimum. What that minimum will consist of depends on the nature of the work. There is always something of a trade-off involved. The choice is between dealing with something quickly at the cost of disrupting the rest of your work, and dealing with it tomorrow in a non-disruptive and orderly way.

Exercise

Every job and situation will have a different degree of balance between the three degrees of urgency. Spend a bit of time now analysing your own work. Look at how much of your *unscheduled* work falls into each of the three categories. What you are looking for is how much of your work *merits* being placed in each category (rather than the category you are actually placing it in at the moment). Write down below an approximate percentage of your unscheduled work that falls in each category. Once you have written your answers, read the notes underneath.

A How much of my work requires an immediate response?
.... per cent
B How much of my work requires a same-day (but not immediate) response? .... per cent

Total: A + B .... per cent

Remainder (work not requiring an immediate or same-day response) .... per cent

Notes

If you have written down a large percentage of your work as requiring an immediate response, then the nature of your work should be in the provision of direct services, e.g. emergency services, child-minding, cooking, shop assistant, cashier, etc. If you are not in this type of work, then you have probably misunderstood what is meant by an immediate response. Go back and reread this chapter again!

If you have shown a large percentage of your work as requiring a same-day response, then you need to ask yourself some very probing questions about why it has such a high degree of urgency. Is it because you are constantly fire-fighting? Is it because systems don't work properly? Is it because you are acting as the long stop for other people's inefficiency? Or could it be that your workplace has a culture of 'instant response' which cannot really be justified? Or does your boss make unreasonable demands? Remember, every item of work that falls into this category is making it more difficult for you to manage your work properly.

If most of your work doesn't fall into the immediate or same-day categories, then you are excellently placed to become extremely well ordered. Remember the formula *Effectiveness = Creativity x Order*. Knowing the correct degree of urgency to give your work is the key step towards increasing your orderliness. Increasing your orderliness will release your creativity so you can achieve maximum effectiveness.

Comment

I frequently get challenged by people who say that they can't possibly wait until tomorrow until they do their work. It's far too urgent. I would have no problem with this if they were in fact dealing with all their work with dispatch.

But when I probe more deeply I usually find that they are dealing with some parts of their work urgently but the rest of their work is well behind. The result of dealing with too many parts of their work too fast is having a detrimental effect on the remainder. The result is an unbalanced response – for any given piece of work there is either an immediate response or no response for ages. What I am proposing is that they standardise their response so that *everything possible* gets actioned the following day. This will in fact greatly speed up their average response time.

If you are like most people you are probably spreading your work in a fairly haphazard manner across a wide variety of response times. Some work gets done immediately. Some gets done today. Some gets done the next day. Some doesn't get done for a lot longer than that. Some doesn't get done at all. There is no particular rhyme or reason why some work gets done in one timescale rather than another.

Rather than this chaotic and unsatisfactory situation, I am proposing in this book that there should be only two days on which your work gets actioned – today or tomorrow. The strong preference is for tomorrow.

Now I am going to show you how to do this. The first thing you need is to learn more about one of the most effective time-management tools – the closed list. This is the subject of the next chapter.

7

Closed Lists

A closed list is a way of applying limits to our work in order to increase our efficiency.

The great advantage of classifying most of your work as 'tomorrow' is that it means you can use closed lists to the fullest advantage. In my illustration about the two car repair yards, Joe Slobb used no closed lists at all. Mick Cool on the other hand used closed lists for everything. This use of closed lists was the main factor in making him far more efficient than Joe Slobb.

I have already gone into some detail about closed lists in the discussion about limits in Chapter 2 – The Principles. A closed list is one way of applying limits to our work in order to increase our efficiency. It is much easier to work off a closed list than an open list. In the Principles chapter I showed how you could use the principle of closed lists in order to clear a backlog.

Now let's examine how to use closed lists in order to control our working day. Most people use very few closed lists to control their work. Instead they tend to rely on open lists. The most common form of open list is the traditional to-do list.

What makes the to-do list into an open list is the fact that anything can be added to it. There is no line drawn at the bottom. You might start off your day with a list of twenty items. As you go through the day you action some of the items, but at the same time you are adding new things on the end of the to-do list. Most people have had the experience of working away all day on their to-do list and ending the day with more items on it than there were at the beginning of the day.

The open list is one of the biggest bugbears in the struggle to get organised. It is virtually impossible to get through your work if you have a constant stream of new stuff coming in. What usually happens is that you cherry-pick whatever happens to be making the most noise at the time and leave the rest 'for later'. The result is inevitably that the unactioned items build up into a backlog.

So an open list is any collection of items that is not closed off to new stuff coming in. It's like a club that is actively recruiting new members. The original membership gets diluted and can be heard complaining about how they hardly know anyone these days!

A closed list is the exact opposite. It is a collection of items that is closed off from any new items coming in. Like a club that accepts no more members, it will gradually fade away as the old members die off.

As we've seen earlier, a checklist is an example of a closed list. In order to carry out a new task it's often a good idea to break the task down into smaller tasks and make a checklist. Notice that the checklist doesn't add to the work involved in doing the overall task. However detailed the checklist, it is still confined within the closed world of the original task. Mick Cool made a checklist for each of the cars that he was servicing. So each of his days consisted of a closed list of cars (i.e. the ones he had booked in for that day) with a checklist for each car. So he just went to the first car, worked his way down the checklist, and then on to the second car and so on. This is in stark contrast to Joe Slobb, who had new cars coming in all the time and had no checklist for each car. The result was that his work was totally haphazard.

Another good example of closed list versus open-list is what happens when you come back from holiday and find you have a computer full of hundreds of emails that have come in while you have been away.

If you deal with these in an 'open-list' fashion, you will deal with the ones that seem particularly urgent or important or attractive, and leave the rest 'for later'. New emails will start to come in and the result is that you never quite catch up. Some of the emails may still not have been dealt with by the time you go on your next holiday.

So what happens if, instead of this, you deal with the email in a closed-list way? How would you go about it? You would download all the email that has come in while you have been on holiday, and then go offline and work intensely to clear the lot in one batch. It may take several hours, but you will probably discover that it takes you much less time to deal with those emails than it would if you hadn't gone away on holiday and had dealt with them as they arrived.

Dealing with emails in closed batches is by far the fastest way of dealing with them. The advantages of batching up items in this way are not just confined to emails. It is always most efficient to group similar items together and deal with them in a batch. If you have ever needed to make a considerable number of telephone calls, you will know that the quickest and most efficient way is to write down a list of all the calls you want to make, and then work your way down the list. If you can't get an answer, you move on to the next item. When you have finished the list you go back round it again and deal with those you weren't able to complete the first time.

Some other everyday examples of closed lists are:

- A checklist for the papers you need to assemble to do your tax return.
- A list of tasks for closing down your office in the evening (e.g. close filing cabinets, turn off computers, switch on alarm).
- A shopping list.

Closed lists like these make working much easier. Mick Cool finds his work much less stressful than Joe Slobb does. Not only that, he gets more done and gives a better service to his customers.

Now let's have a look at one of the most important characteristics of closed lists.

Imagine that you have a completely clear day in which all you have to do is get through a list of twenty items. You are guaranteed no interruptions and that nothing will be added to the list (well, I did say this was imaginary!). None of the items on the list depends on another and none of them is so urgent that it has to be completed before the end of the day.

You can go home just as soon as you've finished the list – but not before.

In your imagination, you can see that the items on the list vary a lot. Some of them are bigger than others, some are more difficult, some are more unpleasant, some are more urgent, some are more important, and so on.

Before you read any further, answer this question: What

is the best order to do the items on the list? Tick the order on the list below that you think would be best:

Most difficult first
Easiest first
Most urgent first
Most important first
Smallest first
Largest first
One you least want to do first
One you most want to do first
The order in which they are written down
Other_____

Which do you think would be best? Answer the question now if you haven't already done so.

When I ask this question in my seminars, I usually get every one of these possible answers from the group.

My answer is, 'It doesn't matter.' As long as you are going to finish the list, it doesn't matter what order you do them in. You can do them in whatever order you find best for you. But note this applies *only* if you are going to finish the list.

If you are not going to finish the list then it does matter – it matters a lot – what order you do them in. The next day you are going to get a new list, and the old list will have to be added on top of it. If this goes on day after day, you will find that it leads to a problem: if you always use the same principle to decide which items you are going to action first, the same items will always tend not to get actioned.

So if you always action the most urgent items first, what happens to the non-urgent items? They won't get actioned until they have become urgent enough to attract your attention.

If you always action the most important items first, what happens to the least important items? They won't get actioned until they have gone wrong and imposed their importance on you.

If you always action the easiest items first, then anything difficult won't get actioned. You can always find more easy items if you run out!

The only way round this is by always making sure that you complete the list. If you do this, the order in which the items are completed is irrelevant. This is why it is so essential not to take on more work than you are capable of dealing with. Your workload needs to be balanced out on a day-to-day basis. Using closed lists makes this much easier to manage, as we will see.

As long as you know that the list is going to be finished, any order will do – assuming that one item doesn't depend on another item being done first. Personally, when I am dealing with a closed list I usually deal with the easiest things first. With a batch of email I will do a first pass to clear the stuff that doesn't require my attention at all. Then I will go through it again getting rid of the easy stuff. A couple more passes, and I will be down to two or three emails that need some considered action. One of the best parts of doing it this way is that the number of outstanding emails gets smaller very quickly.

I have already mentioned backlogs as being one of the problems that can be solved by using the closed-list principle. Every now and then I find that for some reason – usually because I've overscheduled myself – I have got behind on my work and am having difficulty catching up.

This is particularly annoying for me, as normally I am totally on top of my work and hate the feeling of getting behind and the way it starts to drain my energy. After struggling on for a few days, I decide it is time to 'declare a backlog'. I sweep all the outstanding work into a folder called 'Backlog', and start off fresh. The sense of liberation is instant! Of course the backlog folder still needs to be cleared, but I make it into my 'current initiative' (see Chapter 10) and within a few days it is cleared.

If you have ever been seriously in debt, you will know that debt shares many characteristics with backlogs of work. If you think of debt as a backlog of money, you will realise that it can be dealt with in much the same way as any other backlog.

Many people who have a debt problem act in the same way as someone with a backlog of work. They try desperately to pay off the debt, but all the time new expenditure is coming along and the debt just gets larger and larger. So all their efforts never seem to make any difference. In these circumstances, people sometimes go on a relentless hunt for new sources of finance while trying to find some get-rich-quick scheme that will allow them to pay all the debt off. At the same time they continue spending, because every individual item of expenditure seems to be insignificant compared with their mountain of debt. All they are doing is adding fuel to the flames.

Let's apply the closed-list principle to getting out of debt. Just as with a backlog, the first step is to put a lid on the existing debt. This is often very painful, and involves doing such things as cutting up all one's credit cards and determining that you will incur no more debt for any reason whatever. The next step with a backlog is to make sure you can handle the new stuff coming in. In the same way the second step for clearing debt is to cut current expenditure right back so that the budget is balanced. Until this is done, new debt is going to continue to be incurred. Then finally the last step is to start chipping away at the backlog. In the case of debt, this means starting to pay it off. This will take time and determination, but at least it will now be possible. Until the steps are in the right order, it is all but impossible.

Test yourself

Which of these is a closed list?

1 Your car has developed a number of minor faults. None of them is worth the trouble of booking the car into the garage, so you keep a list on your computer of the faults as they occur in order to get them fixed at the next service.

2 You have got very behind with your work and you are due to go on holiday next week. You sit down and make a list of all the things that you have got to get cleared before you go. Everything else is going to have to wait till you get back!

3 You have locked yourself out of the house on a couple of occasions, so you have developed a habit of saying to yourself, 'Money, house keys, car keys' every time you are about to go out.

4 You have made a list of things that you have to get through today. Two or three more things come up during the morning, and you add them to the bottom of the list.

Answers

1 This is an example of a closed list. Although new items are being added until the service is due, no action is taken on any of them until the list has been closed. The distinguishing feature of an open list is that action is taken while the list is still receiving new items.

2 This is a good example of creating a closed list to make it easier for you to concentrate on what really needs doing.

3 You have created a short checklist as an aide-mémoire. A checklist is a form of closed list.

4 This rather depends on how you add the new items. If you just add them in and deal with them on the same basis as the others, then you have an open list. If, on the other hand, you have drawn a line at the bottom of the original list and add the new ones below the line so they get cleared last, then the original list is still a closed list. It is much more effective to use the second method.

In the next chapter we will deal with a very effective method of creating closed lists which ensures that all your work gets done on a day-to-day basis. I call this the mañana principle, or the art of getting everything done by doing it tomorrow.

8

The Mañana Principle

The art of getting everything done by putting it off to tomorrow.

Let's do a little bit of revision here. In the last couple of chapters we have seen that two ways of improving our control over our day are to:

1 Avoid actioning things the same day whenever possible.
2 Make maximum use of closed lists.

These two combine very well together to make what I call the mañana principle – the art of getting everything done by putting it off to tomorrow. Our motto becomes: 'Nothing is so urgent that it can't be put off till tomorrow.'

Of course this saying was originally meant to suggest that nothing will get done because tomorrow never comes. That's not what I am recommending! Instead, I am suggesting that we collect all incoming work items during one day and action them the following day. In other words we are putting in a buffer of one day.

There are many advantages to working this way and the easiest way to show them is to contrast them with the way we normally work.

Mañana principle	Normal way of working
Automatic closed list	No closed list
New items dealt with systematically	New items dealt with at random
Interruptions minimised	Constant interruptions
Easy to plan the day	Planning very difficult
A day's work on average each day	Workload unrelated to one day's work
Easy to diagnose what's wrong if can't keep up with work	Difficult to diagnose what's wrong if can't keep up with work
Can finish your work every day	Never finish your work

What I am recommending that you do is collect one day's work and action it as a batch the following day. The work can be broken up into batches of related types of action, e.g. email, voicemail, paper and tasks.

Let's look in more detail at how to do this:

Email

Email is a major problem for some people, and the importance of dealing with it systematically can't be stressed enough. Unfortunately by its very nature it invites a haphazard, piecemeal approach.

We have already looked at the best way to deal with it: save up incoming emails throughout the day and then deal with them in batches. Using the mañana principle, email will be cleared once a day.

Email has the great advantage that it arrives in one place and ready ordered. This means it is very easy to deal with one day's worth at a time because all email software will allow email to be date- and time-sorted.

Newer versions of Microsoft Outlook have made this even easier than it used to be. I personally use a programme called the Nelson Email Organiser, which works as an add-on to Outlook and deals with filing of email automatically. One of its automatic actions is to put all yesterday's email into a separate folder. I can then set a filter which removes each item from sight as I finish actioning it. This means that my motivation is kept going because the list gets shorter and shorter as I work. Using this method I have greatly reduced the total amount of time I spend on email each day.

Voicemail

You can action voicemail messages in exactly the same way as email by actioning messages the day after receiving them. However, if you answer the phone personally, remember that the urgency of the action that you take depends on the urgency of the contents of the message, not the fact that it is a phone call. Usually it is sufficient to say to callers, 'I'll do that for you tomorrow.' If they know from experience that you really will do it the following day, you are probably doing much better in their eyes than most of the people that they call.

How do you record all the things that you have promised to do tomorrow? You write them down, of course. We will see the best place to do that when we look at tasks in a moment.

Paper

There was a day when office work consisted mainly of 'paperwork'. I can remember when I first started out in the world of work there were no faxes or emails or voicemail, and to make a long-distance phone call one had to go through a special operator. When computers first came in we were all promised that they would lead to the 'paperless office'. All I can say is that the day I bought my first computer was also the day that I started to buy paper by the ream. Nowadays I buy paper in boxes of five reams!

The other great workplace inventions since I started work have been the photocopier and laser and inkjet printers. The result of all this of course is that now we not only have all the new means of communication, we also have even more paper than before.

Paper presents two main problems: actioning it efficiently and filing it. I will give some suggestions on filing in Chapter 15 on systems. In this chapter I will concentrate on how to deal with it efficiently.

Unlike email, paper does not arrive all in the same place in the right order. We tend to think of paper as what arrives in the post. In fact the post may not even be the bulk of the paper that we have to deal with, because paper arrives throughout the day from a wide variety of sources. If you've been to a meeting, you may come back with a briefcase full of it. You may print out email attachments. You may write down notes about a project or an idea. You may come back from a visit to the office suppliers with several paper invoices. You may receive files from other departments. You may have draft correspondence to check before it is sent out.

All this paper has a tendency to spread itself about. If you work from home, it's only too easy for it to end up in separate piles in various parts of the house. The same thing can easily happen in an office setting, though possibly not to quite the same extent. Briefcases have a natural tendency to become a mobile backlog of paper.

The first step towards having paperwork under full control is to have a central collection point for all incoming paper. The easiest way to do this is to have an in-tray to act as that central collection point. Most people already have an in-tray, of course. Unfortunately they tend to use it as a place for storing paper that they haven't got round to dealing with. Most people's in-trays are in effect pending trays. To control paper properly it is vital that the in-tray's key role as a collection point is re-established. There should be nothing in one's in-tray except newly arrived paper awaiting processing as a batch.

If you don't have a proper in-tray you never know what to do with new bits of paper. You don't want to put them in what you call your 'in-tray' because you know that it's really just another pile of unactioned paper. If you don't know what to do with something, it tends to hold up the flow of work and get lost.

Once you have re-established the proper use of the in-tray you have the answer to the question, 'What do I do with this bit of paper?' The answer is always, 'Put it in the in-tray'. Not having an easy answer to this question is the reason why paper has a tendency to accumulate in piles. Now that you know exactly what to do with any new bit of paper that arrives in your life, the tendency for piles to form should disappear.

We don't just put the piece of paper in our in-tray and

leave it there, of course. What we are doing is allowing it to accumulate during the day so that we can action it tomorrow. Just as we collect email for one day and deal with it in one batch the following day, so we collect paper for one day and deal with it in one batch the following day.

With a properly functioning in-tray, it's easy to do this. At the start of each day's work the tray should be empty (see below). After opening the post, you put everything that you haven't thrown away immediately into the in-tray and forget about it. If you come back from a meeting with lots of notes and documents, you empty your briefcase into the in-tray and forget about it. If you write some notes to yourself about a project, you put them in the in-tray and forget about them. If you get some files or papers from another department, you put them in your in-tray and forget about them. If you print out an attachment to an email, you put it in your in-tray and forget about it. If you come back from purchasing some items for the office, you put the invoices in your in-tray and forget about them. If you receive a fax, you put it in your in-tray and forget about it.

Remember what you are doing is collecting one day's worth of paper. At the end of the day (or the beginning of the next day), take all the paper from your in-tray (Tray A) and put it into a second tray (Tray B). Tray B now contains all the paper that came in yesterday and is therefore a closed list which can be actioned as one batch. You are protected from the arrival of new paper while actioning it because all new paper goes in Tray A where you don't need to do anything about it for the time being.

As with email and voicemail, you need to monitor the

paper coming in to check whether any of it is same-day urgent. This is less likely than with email. Remember the rule: it gets dealt with tomorrow, unless there is a significant downside to not doing it today.

Tasks

So far I have shown you how to deal with email, voicemail and paper. These are all incoming messages by various means of communication. If you have any other means of communication (such as instant messaging or text messaging) that form a major part of your work, you can deal with them using the same principles.

These communications cover a large part of our daily work, but far from all of it. We have a plethora of other things to do that can be grouped under the generic name of 'tasks'. This category can broadly be defined as anything we have to do that is not dealing with incoming email, voicemail, paper or other means of communication.

Of course many tasks arise directly from our communications. We may for example receive an email tasking us with writing a report or undertaking a new project. We deal with the email itself along with other emails received the same day. The task arising from it can be dealt with separately under the 'tasks' heading if it's too big to be dealt with as part of dealing with the email. Other tasks may arrive from a wide variety of sources. They may for example be part of wider projects, requests from clients or superiors, promises we have made, or just things that have popped into our heads as needing doing.

Tasks may include relatively simple things that can be done in one go, such as:

Call insurance broker for quote
Tidy desk drawer
Buy birthday present
Order more paper
Arrange interview with John
Email photo to Georgina.

Or they may involve more complicated things, such as:

Arrange presentation for potential clients
Write report on results of West of England branch's
    marketing campaign
Set up new training centre in Birmingham.

These are all things that it would obviously be impossible to do in one go. Rather than calling them tasks, they are better called 'projects'. For my purposes, a project is a collection of tasks leading to a desired result. All projects consist of nothing but a series of tasks. It is almost always possible to convert a task into a project by breaking it down further. A task such as 'write report' becomes a project when we break it down into 'research results', 'write outline', 'write introduction' and so on. Whether you want to make a particular item into a 'task' or a 'project' is decided on the purely practical grounds of whether or not you want to complete it in one go.

If we look at the first list above, you can see that each of them could be broken down further if you wished to do so. This is especially useful if you are pushed for time or if you are experiencing a certain amount of resistance to the item.

115

Look up insurance broker's number
Spend ten minutes tidying desk drawer
Jot down ideas for birthday present
Compare paper prices on-line
Check dates available for interview with John
Scan photo.

Equally, the projects in the second list can be broken down into 'first steps'. Usually the first step with any project is to answer the question, 'What needs to be done now?' The answer to this question will usually produce quite a few individual tasks.

So whether one is dealing with a single small task on its own or with the current steps of a larger project, the same principle of saving the tasks up during the course of one day and doing them the following day can be followed.

Unlike email or paper, tasks have no physical presence. They are just concepts until they are carried out. To give them physical form, they need to be written down. A page-a-day diary is the ideal place to write down tasks. Whenever you are given a task to do or think of one, all you have to do is to write it down under tomorrow's date in the diary. At the end of the day, draw a line under the list to show that it is complete. Then the next day you have a closed list of tasks to complete as one batch.

What about tasks that you decide are same-day urgent? We have already mentioned that the best way to put some distance between yourself and them is to write them down. If you are using a page-a-day task diary, then the obvious place to write them down is on today's date below the line. This means you can then action them at whatever time you think appropriate during the day.

The act of writing same-day tasks below the line on the current day has several advantages:

1 The act of writing them down gives you a buffer which prevents you from reacting to them as though they were immediate tasks.

2 In the act of writing them down you are forced to make a conscious decision about whether to write them down for action today or tomorrow.

3 Since you have drawn a line at the end of the list, anything added below that line represents extra work that you were not expecting. This acts as a discouragement from doing things unnecessarily the same day.

4 At the end of the day you can audit the items that you wrote below the line to check that they really justified being done the same day.

5 If you find that you have a chaotic day, it will almost certainly be because you started doing things that were not written down. Whenever you have a bad day, always ask yourself, 'How many things did I do today that I didn't write down first?'

I will be dealing more fully in a later chapter with how to deal with projects. For the moment it's sufficient to say that there are basically two ways of dealing with a task that's too big to be tackled in one go:

1 You can make it into a project by breaking it down into smaller tasks, as mentioned above.

2 You can recirculate the same task until it is finished.

Recirculating the task adheres to the principle of 'little and often' and so can be very effective. For example, if you were given a week to write a report you might enter 'write report' on your task list for tomorrow. You would then work on it for as long as you wanted that day, and then re-enter the same task again for the following day.

Recirculating tasks works particularly well with reading matter. Many people find it difficult to keep up with reading professional literature. This can be absolutely vital for staying abreast of the latest developments in one's field. Yet the pace of life is such that it is very difficult to find the time. For example, you want to read the monthly *Harvard Business Review*. Put 'read *Harvard Business Review*' as a task on your list every day. Each day you read only the bits that you feel like reading. You will find that by the time the next issue comes out you will have read everything in the magazine that's of interest to you. Don't be tempted to skip the item some days as it's important that you read *something* every day.

An even simpler method with reading material is to recirculate the magazine itself through your in-tray, rather than write it on your task list. When you've read all you want to each day, just put the magazine back in Tray A for the following day. When a new issue comes out, put it in place of the old issue and throw the old one away.

Test yourself

How would you deal with the following?

1 An email arrives with a big attachment, which you are asked to read and comment on before the next

meeting of the advisory board in a month's time.

2 You come back from having lunch with a client. The client has given you several brochures to look at and you also have notes you made during the meeting about action you have promised to take.

3 You need to keep up to date with the weekly *Widget News*. You have about two months' worth of copies that you haven't read, and you need to catch up.

4 When you finish filing some papers in your personal 'Office Policies and Procedures' file, you note that the file is too full to take any further papers.

5 A colleague sends you an email which says, 'You really must look at www.markforster.net. It's a fantastic site.'

6 Your boss asks you to arrange a meeting for the two of you and an important client for tomorrow.

7 You decide that you are going to get your Christmas shopping done early this year.

8 You want to take some major new initiatives in your work, but your ideas so far are very vague.

Answers

1 There is no urgency about this so you don't need to deal with it on the day of arrival (Day 1). Your best course of action is to deal with the covering email the following day (Day 2), along with the rest of the previous day's emails. Print out the attachment and put it in Tray A. The following day (Day 3) you will start reading the attachment and making notes about possible comments. If you don't finish it in one go, put it back in Tray A for further action on Day 4. Repeat this as often as necessary.

2 Empty the contents of your briefcase into Tray A and forget about them for today. The following day (Day 2), start reading the brochures (recirculating as necessary) and extract the action items from your notes to put in your task diary for the following day (Day 3). You can shorten this if necessary by working on the action items straight from your notes on Day 2 as part of clearing Tray B.

3 This is a backlog situation. Put the most recent issue of the magazine in Tray A and either put the rest where you can't see them or throw them away. If you really must catch up with the old magazines, make it into a separate initiative (see Chapter 10).

4 Put 'sort out Office Policies file' in your task diary under tomorrow's date.

5 Put 'investigate www.markforster.net' in your task diary under tomorrow's date.

6 Put 'arrange client meeting' in your task diary below the line on today's list. Action it at a suitable moment during the day.

7 Ask yourself, 'What needs to be done now?' and enter the answers in your task diary under tomorrow's date.

8 Put 'think about work initiatives' as an item for tomorrow in your task diary.

The task diary is capable of doing a lot more for you than just storing items for action the following day. We'll be taking a more detailed look at it in the next chapter.

Summary of the mañana principle

- Collect one day's work and action it the following day.
- Action it in batches of related actions, e.g. email, voicemail, paper, tasks.
- Collect incoming paper in Tray A during the day. Then transfer it to Tray B for action the next day.
- Write down incoming tasks under tomorrow's date in a page-a-day diary ('task diary').
- Draw a line at the end of today closing off tomorrow's list in the task diary.
- Write any 'same-day' items into your task diary below the line on today's date for action at a suitable moment today.

9

Task Diary

You will never get anyone to attach a higher priority to your work than they perceive you are giving to it yourself.

The task diary is a highly flexible tool and can play a major role in helping you to keep track of your work. It is especially useful for helping you to keep track of things that have been passed to other people for action.

For my task diary I use a perfectly ordinary page-a-day diary of the type that can be bought quite cheaply at any stationer's. If you are starting to use the task-diary concept in the second half of the year, you can buy page-a-day diaries that start halfway through the year.

Personally, I don't combine my task diary with my schedule. That's because I don't like the page-a-day format for my schedule. But if you do, then there's no reason why you can't use the same book for both. Just be sure that the scheduled appointments and the tasks don't get mixed up.

My own personal preference is to write my tasks down on paper, and that's what I shall be describing. But if you prefer to record things electronically there is absolutely no reason why you shouldn't do so. Personally I find that writing – with all its accompaniments of crossings out and varieties in ink colour – gives me a better feel for the tasks. Nevertheless, you can easily adapt what I am going to say to such programmes as the task manager in Microsoft Outlook.

So far we have examined how we can use the task diary for the following:

1 Collecting tasks to be dealt with as a batch the *following* day.
2 A convenient place to write down any type of work that we need to action the *same* day.

However, we often get work that is not suitable for actioning either the same day or the following day. For example, we need to phone Tom, and Tom is only going to be around on Tuesday next week. There wouldn't be much point in putting 'phone Tom' down for the following day. The answer of course is to write 'phone Tom' under Tuesday next week's date.

This is an example of using the task diary to schedule an item to a specific date in the future. We want to do this if it has to be done on that date or can't be done *until* that date.

When we action our list of tasks for today, it's therefore going to include items that we:

scheduled for that date some time ago
collected the day before
have written below the line today because they merit 'same-day' action.

This ability to schedule forward makes the task diary an extremely flexible and effective tool. Here are the main uses that I have for my task diary. You may be able to develop other ones for yourself.

- *Reminders* You can remind yourself to take some action on a particular date. This can be very useful for things like buying birthday presents. Most people have their loved ones' birthdays in their diary, but what they frequently do not have is a reminder a couple of weeks beforehand to do something about buying a present and card.

- *Other people's time management* However good your own time management, you are going to be up against other people's poor time management. It is worth remembering that most poor time managers use the Joe Slobb principle of working on whatever catches their attention at the time. You can turn this to your advantage by making sure that it's you who catch their attention more than anything else. The best way to do this is by systematic follow-up. The task diary makes this easy. Whenever you send an email, leave a message, or ask someone to do something, make sure that you put a note in your task diary to follow up after a couple of days. Do the same if someone promises to do something for you. Follow-up is essential because you will never get anyone to attach a higher priority to your work than they perceive that you are giving it yourself.

- *Monitoring* Following up other people is fine, but the person you most need to follow up on is yourself. Schedule regular checks for your projects to ensure that they are developing in the way you want them to. Remember that if you don't pay attention to a project, it will either die or come back and bite you.

- *Thinking* Have you ever had a great idea but weren't quite sure what to do with it? Or perhaps you had someone suggest you do something and you couldn't make up your mind whether it was a good idea or not. Or perhaps you have received a glossy brochure and you are in two minds whether to buy the product. All these are things that you don't want to make any rash decisions about. Instead, have another look at them in a couple of weeks' time, when they may look quite different. Just put a note in your task diary to review them after whatever is an appropriate interval.

• *Scheduling* If you are beginning to build up a backlog of actions, one way you can deal with them is to schedule a few of them each day over a period. That will mean that you no longer have a huge weight of unactioned things hanging over the current day. You have spread the load over a period and that should make you feel far less burdened.

As you can see, the task diary is a very simple but very effective tool. Most of the best tools are simple. Complicated ones tend not to get used. However, there are some tasks that it is better to deal with without using the task diary. These are tasks that we want to do every day, or several times a week. Let's look at them now.

Daily tasks

So far we have looked at what are basically one-off tasks. Most of us, however, will have some tasks that we want to do every day. It would be irritating and time-consuming to have to write these into our task diary every day and so the easiest thing is to keep a separate permanent list of them.

Some examples of the sort of thing that would be suitable for this list are:

Office-closing routine

When you stop work in the evening it is helpful to have a routine for making sure everything is closed down properly. This might include tidying your desk, backing up, putting files away and checking security.

Dealing with things that come in on a daily basis

Many things are dealt with much more easily on a daily basis than by leaving them until they accumulate into a huge block. For example if you deal with your own accounts, you may have an average of two or three invoices a day. These take very little time to deal with on a daily basis, but a huge pile of 900 invoices at the end of the year can be pretty daunting. Another example is the problem many people have in submitting their expense claims monthly or quarterly. If you enter your expenses on the sheet every day, you will find that it takes only a moment and never grows to the stage where you start to resist it. Similarly, any sort of log or daily record, such as a record of billable hours, is best kept up to date on a daily basis.

Things we want to do every day

On the little-and-often principle there may be many things that we want to do a bit of every day. Examples might be reading, exercising, writing and so on.

Rotation

Some things are best dealt with on a rotation basis. Instead of doing the whole task every day, you do a bit of it each day. Often this can be done on a weekly basis. So you might have a house-cleaning routine – clean the sitting-room on Mondays, the kitchen on Tuesdays, etc. You might apply the same principle to the drawers and cupboards in your office. You might have a rule that you weed one file every day in your filing system.

The daily task list is not by any means limited to the examples I have given above. You can think up your own things. Beware of putting large items on this list, because ideally you want to be able to get through the whole list quickly. You should see it as a collection of easy tasks that you are looking forward to because they spell the end of the day's work rather than a huge pile of difficult things that you are dreading throughout the day.

Test yourself

How should you deal with the following?

1 You have a brilliant idea in the shower about a new product. In the past you have often had ideas in the shower but usually fail to do anything about them, so they have been forgotten.
2 You have a lot of projects on hand. Because you are very busy, once you have completed the current actions for a particular project you have a tendency to forget about that project until the next action is due. Unfortunately this often results in things going wrong without your noticing.
3 You tend to forget your wedding anniversary (or other important anniversary) because you don't look at your diary until the beginning of the day, and it's too late by then!

4 You leave a message on a colleague's voicemail asking for some information. You do not need this information for a couple of weeks.

5 You have overscheduled yourself over the last few weeks. Today you have several hours to catch up but you have so much to do that you don't know where to start.

6 You want to write a weekly email newsletter.

Answers

1 The important thing is to record the idea before you forget it. You can write it down in a notebook or on a scrap of paper, or record it on an audio recorder. But however you do it, your aim is to get it into your task diary under the heading 'Think about . . .'

2 It's a good idea to programme reviews of all your projects into your task diary.

3 Put a reminder about two weeks beforehand into your task diary.

4 The fact that you don't need the information for a couple of weeks means that you may not bother to chase up your colleague until the information is needed urgently. That will be too late. Instead, put a reminder in your task diary for a couple of days' time to check whether you have received the information you need.

5 The easiest way of dealing with a backlog of actions like this is to schedule them forward in your task diary. Do the most urgent ones today and spread the rest over a number of days, or even weeks. And don't forget to make a resolve not to overschedule yourself in future – if you don't leave enough time to do your work no system in the world is going to be able to cope with it!

6 Put 'write newsletter' on your daily task list. It's much easier to write a weekly newsletter in daily instalments than to try to write it all in one day. Do a bit every day and the newsletter will virtually write itself.

10

Current Initiative

It is surprising how easy it is to forget that the way to get things done is to do them.

So far we have looked at how to deal with email, voicemail, paper, tasks and daily tasks. These constitute most of our daily work apart from meetings and other scheduled items. These are all, however, basically reactive in nature. In order to take our work forward we need to allocate some time to being proactive.

Here I am going to introduce a concept called the current initiative. If you allow it to, it will take your life and business forward in a way you never imagined possible. It will enable you to turn pipe dreams into reality.

The idea behind the current initiative is that you start work every day by concentrating on one selected initiative. By focusing on one thing in this way you can move much faster than you could if you incorporated the actions relating to it into the task list.

My definition of the current initiative is 'what you do first every day'. It is what you do every day before you start on your email, voicemail, paper, tasks and daily tasks. This is a priority spot that is designed to be given only to those things that are important for the future.

Let's break down the definition 'what you do first every day' a bit further. There are three parts to it:

1 Do
2 First
3 Every day.

Let's deal with each of those in turn.

You need to do something

This sounds like a statement of the blindingly obvious, but it's surprising how easy it is to forget that the way to get things done is to do them. As an example of this, I have coached quite a few PhD students over the years. They often come to me because they have got stuck over writing their thesis. The first question I usually ask them is, 'How long is it since you last did any work on your thesis?' The answer is usually weeks ago, months ago or even in extreme cases years ago. I tell them that the reason they are stuck is that they haven't done anything, not the other way round. I encourage them to do *something*, however small, towards their thesis every day, and usually that is sufficient to get them moving again.

Another example of people getting stuck because they don't do anything is the filing of tax returns. In the United Kingdom, tax returns for self-employed people are due in by a deadline of 31 January. Every year many thousands of people send their tax returns in at the last possible moment, or are a few days late and get an automatic and completely unnecessary fine. Every year accountancy firms get swamped in January by desperate clients trying to get their accounts sorted out in time to submit the return. Now why is this? Is there any reason why it's easier or better to do your tax return in January rather than September the previous year? No, no reason at all. They just haven't got round to doing anything about it.

I myself always wanted to see the great ballerina Sylvie Guillem dance, but somehow I just never managed to get round to it. Finally at the beginning of this year I realised that if I didn't see her soon it would be too late. So at last I decided to *do* something about it and as a result we were present as she received a standing ovation for one of her greatest performances of *Manon*.

For almost any initiative, the route to success is regular, focused *action*. I can't guarantee that you will succeed at everything you apply this rule to, but even if it doesn't work out you won't need to blame yourself for failing to put in the effort.

How much work do you need to do each day in order to keep an initiative going? My answer is you need to do 'something'. It really doesn't matter how much you do on any given day as long as you do something. Doing something keeps the initiative alive. Doing nothing lets it die.

If you do something every day, some days you will do a lot and some days you will do a little, but either way you will be engaging with the initiative. If you want a precise time to aim for, you can give yourself the goal of doing at least five minutes' work on it. Ninety per cent of the time you will go on to do more than five minutes – sometimes you will do much more. But even if you do only the minimum five minutes, it doesn't matter. You have chalked up a success.

So there's the first element for the current initiative: it's what you *do* first every day.

You need to do it first

I discovered long ago that if I really want to get moving on something during a particular day – especially if it's something challenging – it is of the utmost importance that I do it first thing. I need to make a start on it before anything else has a chance to get in the way. The sort of things we are dealing with as current initiatives are, by their very nature, things that we are likely to resist doing. They may be things that we have been putting off for a long time already. Or they may be things that take us out of our comfort zones.

Consider the following scenario. You have been putting off getting moving on a big report that you are supposed to be writing. You decide that the following day you are going to devote three hours to writing it. The next morning you come into the office full of the intention of working for three hours solid . . . you decide that you will make yourself a cup of coffee before you start . . . then you think it would be a good idea to check your email in case there's anything that needs a quick reply . . . you're just finishing that when it occurs to you that you'd better check that your boss doesn't have anything urgent for you either . . . and you'd better have a word with Bill because he's just back from the States today and might have some important points . . . and you mustn't forget to say 'Hi' to Jane because it's her birthday . . . and . . . Good heavens! It's four o'clock already. No point trying to work on the report now. You decide that tomorrow without fail you'll work on it for three hours . . . which, strangely enough, is exactly what you said yesterday too.

Contrast that with what happens if you decide that you are going to work on the report for at least five minutes before you do *anything* else. You come into the office, switch on the computer, open the file and start typing.

Who is more likely to get the report done first?

Remember, if you don't work on your chosen initiative first thing, before everything else starts to crowd in on you, you will have great difficulty in getting moving on it. The remedy is to make time for it before you even look at anything else. Don't worry about all the other things you have to do; they will all find their own level.

That completes the second element of the current initiative: it's what you do *first* every day.

You need to do it every day

I have already written quite a bit in earlier chapters about the advantages of doing things little and often. Doing something every day is the way to ensure that it progresses. It's up to you of course to decide what you mean by 'every day'. You may mean seven days a week. More likely with a work-related initiative you will mean five days a week. Whether you work at it seven days a week or five days a week doesn't matter, just so long as you are working at it on every qualifying day.

You will be sure of doing this only if you remember the two previous conditions. All you have to do is 'something', but you need to do it 'first' before anything else. It's easy to make the mistake of setting yourself too big a goal for the day and then failing to get started because you are overawed by it. Think back to the example I gave of setting yourself the task of working for three hours on your report. Because three hours' work is quite daunting it's only too easy to procrastinate all day. But if you have set yourself the task of doing only at least five minutes' work on it, you will find it much easier to get moving on it right at the beginning of the day and to keep this going every day.

It's easy to find an excuse for not doing an hour's work on something. But what excuse is valid for not doing five minutes' work on something?

There may of course be days on which you are away for the entire day and it would really be impossible to do any work on your initiative. This doesn't matter, because your commitment is to work on it every *available* day. It's essential though to identify non-available days in advance. It's no good getting to the day and then deciding you won't have any time for the initiative. Your mind will mark that down as a failure. If you've given yourself permission in advance not to work on a particular day, your mind will accept that and not consider it a failure. Remember, as far as your mind is concerned failure breeds failure and success breeds success. If you want to succeed at something big, the secret is to give yourself lots of small successes on the way.

Whatever your initiative is, if you work on it every day without fail it will progress. Working on it every day is far more important than how long you work on it. In the same way, I do not recommend you to set a target time for the current initiative. Work on it for as long as you feel able, and you will find that some days you do a lot and some days you do a little – but overall you will advance faster than you thought possible.

So that's the third element of the current initiative: it's what you do first *every* day.

Test yourself

What would be the best goal to set yourself each day in these situations?

1 You want to go for a three-mile run every morning before work without fail.
2 You want to learn French for at least an hour every day.
3 You want to telephone five new contacts every day.

Answers

1 Remember that if you want to do something every day, then it is fatal to set too large a goal. Otherwise sooner or later a day will come when the thought of doing it that day will be too much for you. In this example, if you set yourself a goal to run for three miles every morning there will definitely come a day when the rain is being blown horizontal by the wind and nothing is going to get you out of bed and into the bad weather. Even if you get yourself running but go for only two miles instead of three, you will have failed. I suggest your goal should be to get outside the front door wearing your jogging kit. Once you have got that far, you will probably go for a run. There may be some days you will turn right round and go back indoors, but even then you will have chalked up a success.
2 The thought of doing an hour's French is going to be

too much for you some days. So your goal should be to do *some* French, preferably at a specific time in the evening. However much or little you do, your mind will register a success provided you have done *something*.

3 Making telephone calls to new contacts is a high-resistance activity for most people, and any excuse is good enough not to do it. I suggest you make it your goal to identify five contact names and write them down with their telephone numbers each day. Remember that it's your primitive mind that provides the resistance. Your rational mind still intends to call the numbers, so you should find that once you have written the list you progress naturally into calling the numbers.

You may be asking how many current initiatives you can have going at one time? Well, to answer that let me ask you a question: 'How many things can be done *first* every day?' The correct answer is 'one'. To get the proper effect of the current initiative, you can only do them one initiative at a time. But don't worry that doing them one at a time will be slow – it's actually quicker to do them that way.

Another question you may be asking is, 'How long should something remain my current initiative?' The answer is, 'Until it's finished'. You need to make your own definition of what 'finished' means – and you need to do it before you start on the initiative.

Before we look at this in more detail, let's have a look at the sort of things that the current initiative is designed for. You are of course free to use it for anything that you like, but my experience leads me to believe that there are three main areas in which it is best used. These are:

1 Clearing backlogs.
2 Sorting out defective systems.
3 Getting projects up and running.

Let's look at these in turn.

Clearing backlogs

If you have any significant backlogs of work, I recommend that you make clearing them into a current initiative as early as possible. The reason for this is that backlogs are a very big energy drain. If you have a serious backlog of work, it will be affecting everything you do. Clearing a backlog gives such a great sense of liberation and energy that it is well worth making it among the first things that you do.

Clearing a backlog is ideally suited to being the current initiative. Working at it first thing every day can make huge inroads into the backlog very quickly. That is, of course, provided that you have closed the backlog properly.

Whenever I find that I am getting behind, the temptation is to struggle on trying to clear it. This usually means that I get further and further bogged down. I've now learned that it is far better and easier to declare a backlog, and move all the material I am behindhand with out of my sight to be dealt with as separate project. Then I start afresh with the new stuff coming in. Doing it this way means that I can be instantly up to date. Of course I mustn't forget to look at the reasons why I got behind in the first place; otherwise I will continue to build up one backlog after another.

My advice, therefore, is that the top priority for the current initiative should be to clear any outstanding backlogs. This will release your energies for the rest of your work. Clearing backlogs feels just like getting out of debt. Suddenly you are back on top and dealing only with current stuff. The sense of freedom is almost palpable.

Sorting out defective systems

After getting rid of any backlogs, the next thing to consider for the current initiative is to sort out any defective systems that are getting in the way of your work. Your work systems should be supporting your work. If they are defective, they will always be acting as a brake on your effectiveness. It is quite easy to tell when a system is defective. You will find yourself saying things like, 'I *never* know where to put these' or 'They *always* go missing'. The key words are *never* and *always*. When things are going wrong on a continual basis, you can be sure that there is a malfunctioning system at the bottom of it.

The degree of difficulty involved in sorting out a system will vary enormously. Some systems need only a bit of thought to put them right. For example:

Q. Why does paper always spread itself all around my house and office?

A. Because I don't have a central collection point for incoming paper.

139

Other systems may require a considerable investment of time, energy and money to get right. This investment is, however, almost always worthwhile. When a small business starts out, its major constraint is usually how many customers it can *get*. Once it starts to become successful, the major constraint will change to how many clients it can *handle*. The number of clients a business can handle is largely a function of how good its systems are. A small business that has not got to grips with its systems at this stage is likely to find itself in serious trouble.

The right time to set up a good system, of course, is *before* you need it. However, none of us is so perfect that we anticipate everything, so we need to keep a constant eye on identifying those aspects of our business that are going wrong. Once you have identified a malfunctioning system, put it on your list to become the current initiative. The exception is if it would take so little time to sort it out that it could be dealt with as a simple task. You will find that the time invested in sorting out systems malfunctions is repaid many times over.

Getting projects up and running

The current initiative is not to be confused with a project. Most of your projects can be dealt with perfectly happily without ever becoming the current initiative. There is a whole chapter later on in the book about how to deal with projects from the point of view of your personal time management.

However, some projects need a period of concentrated attention to get them *up and running*. This particularly applies when you are trying to get something new started.

Personally I have used the current initiative slot for such things as getting my website up and running, revamping it at a later stage, getting a spring programme of seminars off the ground, putting together a book proposal, doing my tax return, writing a new constitution for a voluntary committee, and introducing a new charging structure for coaching clients. Without the current initiative, I might have continued thinking about some of these for ages without doing anything about them.

There is one type of project for which the current initiative is not suited. That is any project that consists of repetitive actions over a long period. The sort of projects that fall into this category include such things as learning a language, writing a book, keeping fit, practising an instrument, studying for a qualification and so on. I will be describing how best to deal with these in Chapter 14.

Test yourself

Which of the following are suitable for being the current initiative?

1 It is January. Your boss tells you that this year he wants you to organise a summer ball for the firm's major clients. This is going to be quite a lavish affair, with invitations going to local bigwigs as well as clients.
2 You are going on holiday to France next year, and you decide you would like to improve your usual pathetic performance at speaking French.
3 You run your own business. You find yourself saying, 'I really must do something about getting more clients, but I never seem to be able to find the time.'

4 You have just introduced a new product line, and a new client makes a major order.

5 You are way behind on the designs for the new catalogue.

6 You have just spend half a day searching for the notes that you made at a client meeting two months ago.

Answers

1 You need to put in quite an effort at the beginning of this project in order to get it up and running. You could make it your current initiative to plan it, set up a committee, negotiate a budget, research the invitation list, decide the venue, etc. Once this initial phase has been completed, the project will still generate work but this can be dealt with on an ongoing basis using the task list. When the summer ball gets closer, you may need to make it your current initiative again for a while to progress it further.

2 Learning a foreign language is a repetitive project and is not suitable for being a current initiative. See Chapter 14 for how to handle it.

3 It is prime material for a current initiative to get a marketing/sales plan up and running.

4 You should already have put in place all the systems necessary to deal with this before the product was launched. So this should not qualify for a current initiative at this stage unless you find your systems are woefully lacking.

5 Exactly the sort of thing the current initiative slot is designed for.

6 This is a systems malfunction. You need a current

initiative on sorting out your filing system so it can properly support you in finding things.

> ### Here is an example of one of my own current initiatives
>
> I'd decided that I wanted to run some more seminars but had not yet got round to deciding what form they would take or when they would happen. So I made the subject into a current initiative.
>
> - *Day 1* Sent email to booking secretary of hall in which I usually hold the seminars, asking what dates were free in December and January. Reply received same day.
> - *Day 2* The December dates were not suitable so decided on two dates in January. Sent email booking them.
> - *Day 3* Decided on price, timings, etc. for seminars. Put an announcement of the dates in newsletter due to go out in two days' time.
> - *Day 4* Put details on website.
>
> The seminars have now reached the 'up-and-running' stage. Bookings will now start to come in but they will be dealt with as current work. I can pass on to a new current initiative.
>
> There will of course be lots more to do in respect of the seminars, but this can all be dealt

with as current work. When it gets to the stage of detailed design of the seminars closer to the event, I may want to make them my current initiative again for a short time.

11

Will Do v. To Do

Each and every day our aim is to cross off every item from the list.

Let's take stock a bit now and see how what we have been discussing compares with the traditional to-do list.

Most people have experienced the problems to which the traditional to-do list is liable. The list tends to grow faster than we succeed in crossing the items off. There is always a big chunk of items that gets transferred from day to day without ever getting done. Very often it is the more difficult and challenging items that get left. These are likely to be the very items that will take your business or your work forward. A to-do list is a prime example of the difficulties involved in working with an 'open-world' list.

The to-do list is an open list of things that we *might* do during the day. What we really need is a closed list of things that we *will* do during the day. Each and every day our aim is to cross off every item from the list. In order to do this it is obvious that we will have to consider really carefully what exactly needs to be done and how much time we have available to do it. We would not allow ourselves to do anything that did not appear on the list unless it really justified being actioned that day.

I call this type of list a 'will-do' list in contrast to the 'to-do' list. The most important difference between the two types of list is that the will-do list is a closed world. Once we have decided what we are going to do during the day, we do not add to it – or at least not until we have finished the list. In accordance with what we have already learned about closed-world lists, we should be able to work through the list much faster than through a conventional to-do list.

Will-do list	To-do list
Closed list	Open list
What one will do during the day	What one selects from to do during the day
Aim to complete each day	Not completed each day
Made up of subordinate closed lists	Individual unrelated items
Nothing added without a good reason	New items continually added
Current items only	Items of various ages
Similar items batched together	Items in any order
Efficient	Not efficient

The will-do list is based on a simple structure, consisting of the closed lists we have been discussing:

1 Current initiative
2 Email
3 Voicemail
4 Paper
5 One-off tasks
6 Daily tasks

Let's have a look at how this might be applied in practice.

Here is an abbreviated and edited version of my own list for today. You can see from the numbers which of the above sections each item has come from.

- Sort bookshelves (1)
- (Yesterday's) email (2)
- (Yesterday's) voicemail (3)
- (Yesterday's) paper (4)
- Write seminar advertisement (5)
- Seminar details on website (5)
- Prepare tomorrow's appointments (5)
- Decide whether to run teleclasses in December (5)
- Buy birthday present for N (5)
- Write profile page for amazon.com (5)
- Update news items on website (5)
- Find visitors' book (5)
- Obtain visa for NZ trip (5)
- Pay for tickets (5)
- Write minutes of committee meeting (5)
- Write newsletter (6)
- Back up (6)
- Subscriptions (6)
- Tidy desk (6)
- Tidy floor (6)
- Web stats (6)
- Next day's list (6).

In practice, I keep a standard list on my computer, which I run off every day. It contains the main headings, plus the daily tasks (since these are the same every day). For the other tasks I refer to my task diary for the day. What I actually print off each day looks like this:

Will-do list

Current initiative
Email
Voicemail
Paper
Task diary
Write newsletter
Back up
Subscriptions
Tidy desk
Tidy floor
Web stats
Next day's list

The entries in my task diary for this particular day look like this:

Write seminar advertisement
Seminar details on website
Prepare tomorrow's appointments
Decide whether to run teleclasses in December
Buy birthday present for N
Write profile page for amazon.com
Update news items on website
Find visitors' book
Obtain visa for NZ trip
Pay for tickets
Write minutes of committee meeting

The will-do list is made up mainly of items (email, paper, tasks, etc.) that came in yesterday. Therefore it represents a day's worth of incoming work. This means that it is both realistic and necessary to complete this within a day. The list can be done in any order, except that the current initiative should always be done first and next day's list last. In practice I find it best to do the main headings in the order shown, but I usually do the items within the subordinate closed lists in the order of easiest first.

What happens if I know I'm not going to be able to complete the will-do list tomorrow because I am not going to have time? This might happen if I am going to have an exceptionally busy day with regard to meetings or travel.

The answer is that I draw up the list as normal and do as much of it as I can. I carry the rest forward to the next day. In practice this means I need to carry forward only the undone items in my task diary. If adding these to the following day's tasks makes too long a list, I might decide to spread some of the least urgent ones over the next few days, rather than put them all in the one day.

Since the first item on my will-do list is the current initiative, I will aim to get that done even if I have only five minutes available. It may sound insignificant, but it is surprising what a boost it gives to achieve my goal of doing something every day towards the initiative even when time is short.

For the communications items (email, voicemail and paper) my batches will consist of two days' worth instead of one day's. Surprisingly enough, this usually doesn't take much longer to deal with.

For the daily tasks, I simply pick them up again. There's no need to try to catch up with the missing day.

This sort of catching up works fine and causes no problem as long as I remember that the aim is to finish the list every possible day. If I find myself not completing the list on an average day, then I need to do something about it. If I don't, I will no longer be working on a closed-list basis. I will effectively be back in an open-list situation with all the problems that it entails.

When I am away from my workplace for whatever reason, it is very important to make sure that I have left enough time over the following days to catch up. I always keep firmly in mind that if I overschedule myself I will never be able to keep up with the unscheduled work.

If I do find that I am falling behind, what can I do about it? We have already looked at the diagnosis procedure in outline in Chapter 4. We will look at it in more detail in the next chapter.

Test yourself

How would you incorporate the following items into your will-do list?

1 You come back from holiday to find you have around a thousand emails in your inbox, loads of phone messages and an in-tray full of unopened correspondence.
2 You have a habit of forgetting to check your filing cabinet is locked before leaving the office.
3 An email arrives with a huge attachment that you have to read and reply to within the next few days.
4 Your daughter's school rings up to say she is feeling ill and could you please come and take her home.

5 You go away for a weekend training course and come back with loads of ideas that you want to implement in your work.

6 You get a brilliant idea for a new product, but don't quite know what to do about it.

7 Your boss says, 'You know that report I said I wanted next week? Well, things have changed and I need it by close of play today.'

8 You are reading the daily paper during your lunch break and see a very positive review of a new play. You decide you would like to go and see it.

Answers

1 The best way to deal with a holiday backlog like this is to make it into your current initiative. Decide that this is what you are going to do before you go on holiday. That means that the first thing you do on your return to work is to start tackling the backlog.

2 Make this the last item on your daily tasks every day.

3 Print out the attachment and recirculate it through your in-tray until you have finished the action necessary on it.

4 This is a genuine emergency. All you have to do is to get on with it. You do not need to put it on your will-do list at all.

5 Put an item into your task diary: 'List action from weekend training course'. If you are canny, you will have put the item in the diary *before* you go on the course so it is on Monday's list of tasks.

6 Schedule an item in your task diary for a couple of weeks' time to look at it again.

7 Write the action needed below the line in your task diary under today's date, and get on with it as appropriate. (Remember all 'same-day' items must be written down.)

8 Put an item in your task diary for tomorrow to book a seat.

12
Completing the Day's Work

If you are one of those people who claim you work best under stress, then you probably suffer from low processing power.

Throughout this book I have stressed the importance of getting *everything* done. We can't get everything done unless we have a clear definition of what 'everything' is. We also can't get everything done if we don't make sure that we work through to completion each and every day.

With traditional time management it is, as we have seen, virtually impossible to identify what 'everything' is in the context of a day's work. Since traditional time management gives us no definition of 'everything', we have no way of telling whether we have done 'everything' or not. If we are unable to tell whether we have done 'everything', it's impossible to work through to completion.

All this makes it very difficult to identify what the problem is when we feel that we are falling behind. Since traditional time management gives us no objective measure, we have to rely on our feelings to know whether we are falling behind or not. We have no scale on which we can measure it. We can only sense it by our increasing sense of rush, pressure, overwhelm and stress.

However, when we use the *Do It Tomorrow* methods which I have been describing, we are aiming to do one day's worth of incoming work per day. Each day we collect the work that comes in throughout the day and action it the following day. There may also be a need to action some urgent work the same day. So each day's work consists of work that has come in either the same day or the day before. This gives us a completely objective measure of what 'everything' is. We know we are up to date if we have finished the current day's work and have no backlogs of work. We may fall a day or so behind on occasions, but we should be able to catch up quickly. If we can't keep up, we know something is wrong. Because of the way in which the work is organised, we can put our finger precisely on how far behind we are.

My own rule is that if I have not caught up completely within three days at most, I will initiate a diagnostic procedure. This procedure is easy, though the action resulting from it may not be. As we saw in Chapter 4, if you cannot keep up with your work there can be only three things wrong:

1 You are not working efficiently.
2 You have too much to do.
3 You are not leaving enough time.

We looked at what each of these entails in that chapter. Now I want to look in more detail at what we can do about it if one or more of these apply.

Lack of efficiency

What we are talking about here is your basic processing speed. In mechanical terms, are you able to process work as fast as it comes up? If you work in an unplanned and unfocused way, if you are continually being distracted, if you have no sense of purpose, if you are being continually dragged down by backlogs of work, then you are not going to be working efficiently. Your processing power is going to be very low. People whose processing power is low can often only be galvanised into action by the stressful effect of looming deadlines and angry clients. If you are one of those people who claim that you work best under stress, then you probably suffer from low processing power. Someone who has low efficiency will usually fall even further behind when they have very little to do because they don't have the motivating effect of time pressure.

Remedy

The remedy is to use the methods outlined in this book. Work in closed lists and batches of similar actions. That will help you to concentrate and cut down on distractions. The thing you need to watch above all else is that you do as few things as possible that aren't on your list for the day. Keep asking yourself the question, 'How much did I do today that I didn't write down?' Remember that working this system is a skill, and like any skill it needs practice.

Too many commitments

It is important of course to be as efficient as you can be. But there is a limit to how efficient any individual person can be. I believe the tools in this book are the most effective ever developed for improving your efficiency, but even they can't help you to fit a quart into a pint pot once you have reached your upper limit.

The tendency is to think that if you have too much work, you can 'prioritise' your way out of the problem. But let me tell you straight: *you can't!* All that prioritising achieves is ensuring that some of your work never gets done. If you have too many commitments it's not your priorities that are wrong – it's the fact that you have too many commitments. If you have the right number of commitments then prioritising becomes irrelevant. You are going to do the lot, so importance is irrelevant to the order in which you do them.

Remedy

If you have too much work, it's coming from too many commitments. So the place to look is at your commitments. This may be a difficult process, requiring many hard decisions and unpleasant negotiations. But there is no way round it. If you have too much work, you can't get it all done – it's as simple as that!

Remember, the key is to concentrate on the real work – the stuff that is going to take your business or your job forward. Concentrate too on the work that only you can do. And keep asking yourself the difficult questions, like: 'Should I be doing this at all?' 'What is my job really about?'

Not enough time

It's surprising how many people overschedule themselves and then find that they can't get everything done. With meetings it's not just the time involved in the meeting itself that matters. There's also preparation and travel time, of course. But an even bigger factor is that meetings tend to generate work. Sometimes this is essential work and it is important that you do it. The downside is that it is extremely easy to take on commitments in the heat of the moment at a meeting – ones which you would never have allowed yourself to take on if you had had time to consider them properly.

Remedy

People tend to overschedule because they look at the clean white pages in their diaries in a few weeks' or months' time and think that they are empty. But they are not empty – they are already full of all the unscheduled stuff that has to be done. Remember that, when you are agreeing appointments and meetings. It is a good idea to have a rule that you leave a certain minimum amount of time unscheduled during the week.

My methods will give you a pretty good idea of how long it takes to action your incoming work. Make sure you leave time for it every week. If you are away for an extended period, don't schedule any appointments for immediately after your return.

Don't schedule any meetings unless you are sure that they are justified. The meeting must justify itself with respect to the cost of the time of the people attending. Your own presence at the meeting must also justify itself.

I was intrigued when I took a course recently for people intending to do business in Japan. We were taught that one of the stereotypes that the Japanese have about the British is that we have endless meetings at which the only definite decision ever taken is to have a further meeting. Don't allow yourself to fall into the stereotype!

Test yourself

Which of the three possible reasons (low efficiency, too much work, not enough time) is the one *mainly* involved in each of these scenarios?

1 You are the owner of a small business. After several years struggling to build it up, you are now finding it hard to keep abreast of the amount of work. You find yourself constantly rushing around dealing with problems. You are working yourself into the ground but are conscious that you are not making anything like as much money as you should be.

2 You want to leave your current employment and intend to start your own business. Before you can make the jump you want to have your business well established as a spare-time project so that you are not starting from scratch. The problem is that you just don't seem to be able to find the time to get moving on it. Six months after the official launch of your part-time business nothing seems to have happened. You are in despair over the fact that you don't think you will ever be able to leave your job.

3 As one of your department's middle managers, you are on your firm's product advisory committee which meets every two weeks to review the current situation. Every department is represented by someone. The first half-hour is to fix the agenda, and the second half-hour checks which projects need review. After an indeterminate time discussing the projects, everyone is asked if they have any other business. Finally, the date for the next meeting is arranged. You have to allow the

whole morning for the meeting although it is never certain how long it will last. You are also on the firm's publicity advisory committee and the employees' benefits committee, whose meetings are very similar in the way they are run.

4 You are a teacher at a secondary school. You love teaching and are very good at it, but you hate the ever-growing amount of paperwork that you have. You are always behind on lesson plans and marking. This is causing you a lot of stress.

5 You have completely cleared your diary and cut back on all the rest of your work in order to deal with one major project. You find an unexpected problem – with only one major thing to do each day you find it very difficult to get yourself moving. Some days you don't succeed in doing anything at all.

6 You have an open-door policy for your staff and are always ready to help them with any problems or queries that they have with their work. You believe it's important to communicate and keep your staff in the picture so you like to hold email conversations around the office about proposed courses of action. You pride yourself on giving a same-day service to your clients. Unfortunately, in spite of all the encouragement you give your staff, they always seem to have trouble following through on projects. You can't understand why.

Answers

1 *Too much work* This is the classic small-business bind. After having spent years trying to get clients, you now have more clients than you can handle – with the result that you are so busy that you don't have time to see where you are going. This is where you must concentrate on your real work as business owner. Your prime responsibility is for strategy, planning and the setting-up of systems. You must give yourself enough time to carry out this role because no one else can do it for you. Jettison as much of your other work as possible.

2 *Low efficiency* If you ever want to get to the stage where you can leave your job for your own business, you have got to improve your efficiency at your part-time work. Make sure that you give yourself designated hours of work, and that you organise your work in your own business just as well as you organise your work at your employment. Force yourself to push through to completion every day.

3 *Not enough time* These are the stereotypical British meetings. You are there as a 'representative' without any definite role. There is no proper agenda. No effort has been made to identify beforehand what needs reviewing. There is no fixed time for finishing. The meetings are self-perpetuating. You would be well shot of the lot. If you can't persuade your head of department that you shouldn't attend at all, then never go to one of these meetings without an excuse for leaving early, e.g. an 'important client meeting'.

4 *Low efficiency* This doesn't refer to your talents as a teacher. You have low efficiency at dealing with the back-up administration and paperwork. Make sure you incorporate these into a will-do list and work through to completion every day.

5 *Low efficiency* People with low efficiency often need time pressure to keep going and when that is removed they collapse altogether. To increase your efficiency, break the project down into small sub-tasks, schedule them over a period in your task diary, and use some of the methods in the next chapter, 'Keeping Going', to help you to work to completion each day.

6 *Low efficiency* You may be surprised at this answer. But low efficiency it is. You are not only inefficient in yourself, but the cause of inefficiency in others. What you are doing is introducing a huge number of random events into everyone's work, both yours and your staff's. No one can be expected to work efficiently in these circumstances. You are in effect being Joe Slobb (see page 76). Remember that by trying to give an instant response to everyone he provides a far worse service for his customers than Mick Cool does. Look carefully at how you can introduce some buffers into your work and that of your staff.

13

Keeping Going

Lying is an attribute of the rational mind.

Procrastination is largely caused by feelings of being overwhelmed or way behind. When it gets to the stage where nearly the whole of one's work is seen as a threat, the natural reaction is paralysis. When you are on top of your work there is a natural tendency to keep moving, and procrastination occurs much less or not at all. The will-do list keeps you right on top of your work so procrastination becomes much less of a problem. However, it's too much to hope that you will never experience it again, so it's important to look at ways of tackling it.

There are two aspects of procrastination that I want to deal with in this chapter. The first is how to keep moving so that procrastination doesn't happen, and the other is how to get moving again when you do experience procrastination.

Let's start by looking at some procrastination busters.

Working to completion

You can use a variation of the points exercise in Chapter 2 to monitor how well you are working to completion on a daily basis. You score one point every day on which you complete your will-do list. Every day you fail to finish it you lose a point. You are allowed days on which you do not play the game (e.g. if you know you are going to be away), but these must be identified in advance.

Keep a running total and see how high you can get your score in the course of a month. It helps to keep a record of your score in your diary or somewhere else that you can see it.

Don't despise 'childish' scoring games like this. It's surprising how effective they can be in motivating adults as well.

Working in bursts

One of the most effective procrastination busters is to work in timed bursts. These bursts can be any length, but usually will be somewhere between twenty and forty minutes. The more resistance to the task at hand one is feeling, the shorter the bursts need to be. To get moving on a task that one is strongly resisting, it is sometimes a good idea to start with a burst of as little as five minutes and gradually increase the length of bursts.

For example you might be resisting an important writing project. To get moving on it, you start with a burst of five minutes, take a two-minute break, then work at it for ten minutes. You add five minutes to the length of each burst until you reach forty minutes. So the sequence goes 5 – 10 – 15 – 20 – 25 – 30 – 35 – 40 – 40 – 40 – and so on. Once you have overcome your initial resistance, you can standardise on whatever length of burst you find helps you to concentrate the most.

An alternative approach when you have a high-resistance project is to say to yourself that you will work on it for five minutes. At the end of five minutes, you decide if you feel capable of working on it for another five minutes. You can continue doing this until you find that the resistance has dissipated enough to allow you to work normally on the project.

There are a couple of points that need to be stressed about working in bursts. First, the technique is useful both to get you over the initial resistance to a project and to keep your concentration going when you have to work on something over a long period. If you work on something for three bursts of twenty minutes you are likely to get more done than if you do an hour's untimed work on it.

The second point that needs to be stressed is that the effectiveness of the technique depends on stopping when the time is up. If you allow yourself to go on working it dilutes the effectiveness. The more abruptly you stop when your timer goes off, the better. If it's in mid-sentence, better still. The mind craves completion and will want to get back to the task. This helps you to build up a strong momentum.

Working in bursts can easily be used for the different elements of the will-do list. Experiment for yourself to find what works best for you.

Taking breaks

Your day will be much more productive if you programme in some breaks. Just as using timed bursts increases the concentration of one's work, so it also increases the effectiveness of one's breaks. If you have a definite start time and a definite finish time for your breaks you will find they are much more refreshing than if you start the break and finish the break at an indeterminate time.

Lunch break

Don't be tempted to work through lunch. Working through lunch almost always results in your getting less done. This is because your concentration will lapse if you don't allow time to relax. Having lunch and a bit of time to yourself will refresh you positively. The length of your lunch break isn't as important as the fact that you start and finish it at an exact time.

Finishing time

As well as taking scheduled breaks during the day, it is important to finish at a set time. The same applies to your finishing time as to lunch breaks: you get less work done if you *don't* have a definite stopping time. The reasons are the same. Not having proper breaks causes you to lose concentration. Even worse, not having a proper finishing time messes up your private life as well!

Just as the length of your lunch break is your choice, so it's your choice what time you finish work. The important thing is that you stop dead at whatever time you have chosen.

A question I am sometimes asked is: 'What happens when I am working in timed bursts and it gets to the time to take my lunch break? Do I interrupt the timed burst to have lunch or do I put off lunch until I have finished the timed burst?' My answer is that whenever you get an interruption in a timed burst, you should stop the timer and restart it when the interruption is over. This applies both to unforeseeable interruptions, such as the phone ringing, and to scheduled interruptions such as an appointment or lunch break.

Unscheduled breaks

Not all breaks are good for your work. If you take an untimed break, it can easily lead to your being reluctant to get back to work. However, if you find that you are getting tired or your concentration is lapsing, it is usually better to take a break than to try to work on regardless. How can you do this without losing your momentum?

Do you remember what I said earlier about the mind craving completion? You can take advantage of this when taking unscheduled breaks. Our instinctive reaction when we decide to take a break is to work to the next natural finishing point – the end of the next chapter or section or whatever – and then take the break. This seems a very natural thing to do, but the problem with it is that the mind chalks up a completion: 'We've finished!' The mind likes completion, so getting it to start again on the next section can be an effort.

On the other hand, if you stop dead in the middle of something, then your mind is saying in effect, 'But we haven't finished! We haven't finished!' Getting going *[break]* again is much easier because your mind wants to get back to the task to finish it. In fact, while writing the last sentence my timer went off to signify the start of a break. I've marked the spot with *[break]* – as you can see I took it not just in mid-sentence but in mid-phrase!

If you are not working with timed bursts, the best time to take an unscheduled break is when you have just started something new. My rule here is: 'Never take a break until you have started the next thing.' In fact sometimes this works so well that my concentration perks up when I start the next thing and I forget to take the break!

I have often mentioned in this book the positive effects of working on a major task 'little and often'. I have pointed out that it allows the mind to assimilate the progress made. The same applies to shorter breaks. If you come back to a subject after a break – no matter how short – you will find that you have moved on a little. If you don't take breaks you don't get this effect. Breaks don't just refresh you and improve your concentration; they also help you to produce higher-quality work.

Feeling good

Another way *[here I took an unscheduled break in writing – see the previous section]* to improve your general ability to work and keep going is to monitor how good you are feeling. Procrastination, stress, overwhelm and burn-out are all very closely linked and it is difficult to be feeling good when one is suffering from any or all of these.

However, the reverse applies too. It is difficult to be suffering from stress, overwhelm, burn-out and procrastination when one is feeling good. So monitoring one's overall state of mind can have a very beneficial result.

It's very easy to do this. Let's try it now. Stop reading for a second and ask yourself, 'How good am I feeling right now?' Answer by giving a mark out of ten. If you are feeling rather tense and upset you might answer, 'four'. If you are feeling generally on top of things you might answer, 'eight'. You might find it easier to arrive at an answer if, instead of writing down a single figure, you put a double figure like 7/8 meaning 'between seven and eight'. The best answer is the one you give straight off the top of your head. Don't spend time deliberating it.

Try it now. What was your answer? Write it down in the margin or on a piece of paper.

When you did this, you might have been wondering what the definition of 'good' is. I quite deliberately didn't give you a definition. You will only discover what 'good' means for *you* by answering the question, 'How good do I feel?' The more you ask the question, the more you will begin to recognise what it is that you are looking for in order to provide your answer. You will also begin to notice what things in your life tend to affect the score. So don't worry about the definition of 'good'. You will find by experience what the word means for you by doing the exercise. That is better than any definition I could come up with.

Once you have given your answer, do not make any conscious effort to make yourself feel better. All you have to do is observe your feelings. The effect of observing your feelings will be to make you more aware of them, and that in itself will tend to have the effect of improving them.

Ask yourself the question again now. Write the answer down again. Is it the same as the first time or has it changed? You may find that your score has increased already. That will be because you have become more aware. Don't worry if it hasn't!

This technique is very subtle, but also very powerful. It takes time to have an effect. You will probably find if you keep using it that your average score will slowly rise. If you started out feeling three or four, you may find after a few weeks that it has risen most of the time to seven or eight. It may not sound very exciting to have raised a score in this way, but bear in mind that it will have involved your entire mental sense of wellbeing. This can profoundly affect many areas of your life.

I have seen for myself how much it can change things in my own experience. For many years I suffered from a fear of flying caused by having been in a helicopter crash. I was able to cure myself of this fear of flying by using this technique during the couple of months before I was due to make my first flight for eight years. It worked so well in fact that I was able to maintain a score of ten throughout the entire flight, including take-off and landing!

Fooling the reactive mind

There is a whole group of techniques that exploit the fact that it is the rational mind that *provides* the plan and the reactive mind which *resists* it.

What we do in all these methods is to fool the reactive mind into dropping its resistance. How do we do this? We do it by exploiting the fact that the reactive mind is not able to tell when the rational mind is lying to it. Lying is an attribute of the rational mind. The reactive mind doesn't have the concept-making ability that is necessary to tell a lie. Strangely enough, the ability to tell lies is one of the things that distinguish us as humans. Even those other species with the most complex brains have only a rudimentary ability to lie. Our reactive minds don't have the ability to lie and, what's more, they can't recognise a lie – even when they are lied to by other parts of the same person's brain.

We can get the reactive mind to switch off its resistance to a proposed course of action by pretending that we are not in fact going to take the action. Instead, we tell the reactive mind that we are only going to do a relatively innocuous action.

This can be achieved by using the highly effective phrase, 'I'm not really going to [the task] now, but I'll just do [its first step]'.

Here are some examples of this phrase in action:

- 'I'm not really going to write that report now, but I'll just get the file out.'
- 'I'm not really going to ring that irate customer now, but I'll just look up his number.'
- 'I'm not really going to tidy my desk now, but I'll just move that paperclip to where it should be.'

Once you've taken that first action – getting the file out, looking up the number, moving the paperclip – you will have got over the initial step and you may well find that you are hardly even aware that you are moving on to take some additional action.

I can remember, during the summer, sitting in my garden on a Sunday after lunch. It was sunny and very pleasant, and I became aware all of a sudden that the grass needed cutting. Now the last thing I wanted to do was to mow the lawn. So I said to myself, 'I'm not really going to mow the lawn now, but I'll just get the power cable out.' I got up to walk over to the garden shed, and the next thing I knew was that the lawn was mown. Now obviously it had been mown by me, but I had very little memory of actually doing it. Once I got moving on the first step, my unconscious mind took over. It knew perfectly well how to mow the lawn and didn't really need my conscious help!

How does this work?

Your reactive mind sees the task of mowing the lawn or writing a report as a threat. The task may be difficult, or it may take you out of your comfort zone, or it may involve a lot of hard work, or it may stop you doing something else you would rather be doing. This is actually the rational mind's assessment of what the task is going to involve. As usual the reactive mind believes what the rational mind is saying and classifies the task as a threat from which its duty is to protect you.

When the rational mind tells the reactive mind that it's not really going to mow the lawn or write the report now, the reactive mind breathes a metaphorical sigh of relief and lifts the resistance. The threat has been lifted; the reactive mind can relax. There is nothing in the rational mind's assessment of the task that gives the reactive mind the impression that getting the power cable or the file out is difficult. So it sees no need to resist that. Of course the rational mind has every intention of carrying on with the task beyond the initial step, but the reactive mind is not able to see this.

If all this seems a bit far-fetched, then the simplest way to see how it works is to try it. Start with something that you have been mildly resisting, perhaps something like tidying a corner of your office. Say to yourself, 'I'm not really going to tidy that corner now, but I'll just pick up that piece of paper' or whatever is appropriate to the task you have picked. Try it now – and then carry on tidying your office (or whatever your chosen task is) for as long as you feel you want to.

Do it now.

How did you get on? Did you notice how using the sentence caused your resistance to vanish? And did you find that once you had picked up that first piece of paper you carried on almost automatically?

If you have a major task which you are resisting a lot, you may need to use the sentence several times over as you get to each new phase of action, modifying it each time to take you to the next step. It's a bit like people in extreme circumstances saying to themselves, 'I'll just go on to that tree before I collapse' and then, 'I'll just make it to that corner' and so on, maybe keeping themselves going for many hundreds of miles.

Once you have used this sentence for a bit you will probably find that you don't need the second half. By the time you've got as far as, 'I'm not really going to tidy that corner now . . .' you have already started tidying the corner. In fact you may even find yourself saying, 'I'm not going to write the report' and then find yourself writing it. This can be a very powerful way of doing a series of small actions that would provoke a large amount of resistance if done as a whole.

'I'm not going to put that chair away'; 'I'm not going to move that table'; 'I'm not going to get the vacuum cleaner out'; 'I'm not going to make that bed'. You can clean an entire house by telling yourself step by step that you are not going to do it!

'I'll do that later'

A similar way of fooling your reactive mind is by using the phrase 'I'll do that later'. This is particularly useful because when we are tempted to put something off, that is the phrase that usually comes into our minds. If we use that phrase as a way to get rid of resistance, we can apply it to almost anything that comes up.

If for example your office is untidy, this is because you have failed on hundreds of occasions to take the minute action of putting something where it should be. Why did you fail? Because each time you mentally said to yourself, 'I'll do that later.' If we can turn that phrase around so it has precisely the opposite effect, then we have cut one of the roots of untidiness.

As we have seen, there are many occasions on which it is right to do something later. In fact trying to do too many things immediately is one of the prime reasons for disrupting our day with random actions. So how does our mind know, when we use 'I'll do that later', whether we really intend to do the action immediately or not? The answer is that it does know. Remember, the rational mind is using the technique to fool the reactive mind. The rational mind knows quite well whether it intends to do the action or not.

'I'll just . . .'

Another way of abbreviating 'I'm not really going to write the report now, but I'll just get the file out' is to use the second half of the sentence, i.e. 'I'll just get the file out'. This is also very effective, though in my experience it doesn't have quite the power of 'I'm not going to write the report'. You might like to experiment and find out which works better for you.

Positive fooling

If you can fool the reactive mind with a negative when you do want to do something, you may also find that you can fool it with a positive when you don't want to do something.

For instance, if you are on a diet and you are overcome by the impulse to eat a slice of delicious chocolate cake, just say to yourself, 'I'm going to have a slice of cake' – and then don't. Because the reactive mind has been assured that you are going to eat the cake, it will switch off the impulse to eat it.

Although this can be effective, the problem with it is that the cake is still there. You have not removed the source of temptation. This is in contrast with getting yourself to do something, where once the action has been taken it has been taken. As a result it's never likely to be as effective a technique in the long term. However, it's still useful and you might wish to experiment with other ways of using it.

Getting back into the swing

So far we've been looking at ways of preventing or overcoming procrastination. Most of the time these techniques will be sufficient to keep you going until you have completed your will-do list each day. But inevitably one day you will completely fail to get through your list and the whole thing will be in danger of collapsing.

This is as inevitable as falling off when you are learning to ride a bicycle, so you must know what to do in order to get going again as quickly as possible.

The key to recovery is to put your focus in the right place. It's no use berating yourself for being a pathetic failure. That will achieve nothing except to make you feel even more incapable. What you need to focus on above all is keeping the structure in place. The way to do this is to produce a will-do list for the following day. However terrible a day you may have had, this is the way to prevent the next day from being just as bad.

If you don't produce a will-do list for the following day, what will probably happen is that you will just start doing things at random. The list never gets produced as a result and you have another terrible day. Before you know it you are right back where you started. You will have changed virtually overnight from being Mick Cool back to being Joe Slobb!

Remember, it is structure that produces behaviour, not the other way round. To change your behaviour back to what you want it to be, you must re-establish the structure at all costs. The temptation is to wait until you are 'doing a bit better'. If you do, you will be waiting for a very long time.

Here's a short step-by-step sequence to re-establish your work structure. If you follow this you can be back on top in no time at all.

- Write out your will-do list and start working on it. Get back to dealing with today's incoming work tomorrow. That will put you back on top of new work.
- If you have got behind on your work, declare a backlog. Make dealing with the backlog into your current initiative. That will put you back on top of the work you already have.
- Go through the audit procedure.
    A Am I working efficiently?
    B Have I got too much work?
    C Have I left enough time to do it?

There is no point in struggling on without going through

175

this procedure because all that will happen is that your work will become more and more random. If you find yourself resisting the procedure, then say to yourself, 'I'm not really going to re-establish the system now, but I'll just print out a new will-do list'.

Test yourself

What might you do in the following situations?

1 Your desk is always untidy. You make lots of resolutions to improve, but never succeed in keeping to them.
2 You have tried every time-management system under the sun. They always seem to work well for a week or so and then collapse.
3 You want to introduce some better systems but need to catch up a bit first.
4 You have trouble getting yourself back to work after lunch.
5 Even though you've been through the audit procedure several times, you still have difficulty getting to the end of the list every day. You seem to run out of steam about halfway through the afternoon.
6 You find that on days when you have less to do than normal the relative absence of time pressure means that you tend to fiddle-faddle around all day.

Answers

1 An untidy desk is not necessarily a bad thing. It is only a problem if it prevents you from working properly. Put 'tidy desk' on your list of daily tasks, which will be sufficient to stop this from happening.

2 This reflects a basic lack of structure. Every time that you fall off the bicycle you are failing to get back on it again. The result is that you go back to working in a random unstructured way. This time, put your focus on the one point that matters – getting the will-do list written out again. Then you can worry about doing the other steps in the sequence.

3 You've got things in precisely the wrong order. Establish the new systems, then you will be in a position to catch up.

4 This is another example of a lack of structure. The remedy is to put a stronger structure in place. The most important thing is to have a definite start time and a definite finishing time for lunch. Carry a timer or alarm so that you keep to it.

5 There are several things you can do about this. One is to make sure that you have a mid-afternoon timed break and a definite stop time. Another is to institute a points system, as described above (see page 162).

6 The solution is to re-establish the time pressure. The easiest way of doing this is to bring forward your finishing time, e.g. by deciding to take the afternoon off. Make sure you keep to the new time!

14

More on Dealing with Projects

I don't believe that anyone consistently prioritises by importance because it's virtually impossible to do so.

So far we have dealt in detail with all the myriad actions that come at us during the course of a day. We have also looked at the current initiative, a method of focusing on one thing that we wish to take forward at a time. We need now to look in more detail at how to deal with projects as a whole, not in the sense of providing a manual on project development, but in the sense of showing how individuals can control the actions that any project demands of them personally.

For the purposes of this chapter, I need to remind you of my definition of a project. A project is any task that will take more than one session to finish. Following on from this, any project can be broken down into tasks, and virtually any task can be treated as a project should you wish.

Anyone in any sort of position of responsibility will have many projects under-way at any one time. For some people the list of projects may seem unending. In the natural order of things, some will get dealt with adequately and some will languish.

Think to yourself for a moment: what would it be like if

you were able to complete every project to your satisfaction? What would it be like if every time you took on a new project you could totally rely on yourself to get it done? What sort of difference would that make to your aims in life?

If you were able to rely on yourself in this way, you would find that projects and goals would develop as you worked on them and new opportunities would arise that you could grasp without the fear that you would let yourself down. You would discover what it means to have real achievement on a consistent basis.

The two types of project

I distinguish between two different types of project. The difference is a purely practical one that derives from the nature of the projects themselves and means that they need to be dealt with in different ways. If you can't make up your mind which type a particular project belongs to, you can experiment to see which way suits it best.

I call the two types of project:

1 Continuous projects
2 Organisational projects

Let's look at what they consist of.

Continuous projects

A continuous project is one that consists of regular repetition of very much the same sort of action over a relatively long period. The actions themselves are often the main point of the project. Examples would be learning a language, practising a musical instrument, getting fit and so on.

In some cases, continuous projects do have a definite future goal, such as completing a book or passing an exam, but the way to achieve the goal still consists of regularly repeating much the same actions over a long period. Sometimes the actions will continue even when the goal has been reached. For example, once you have achieved a language qualification, you might need to continue to study in order to maintain your level of ability – or you might want to go on to a higher level.

As I mentioned earlier in the book, continuous projects are not suitable for the current initiative slot. The reason for this is that they are long-term or permanent projects, which would tie up the slot and prevent any other project from becoming the current initiative.

Since they are repetitive in nature, the best way to deal with continuous projects is to make a daily habit of them by giving them a definite scheduled time during the day. Alternatively, if they will take only a short time each day, you can put them on your daily-tasks list. Avoid gumming up your daily-tasks list with lengthy actions, though.

Continuous projects take up a regular slice of your day on a long-term basis, so beware of taking on more than a few carefully chosen ones.

Organisational projects

Organisational projects consist of a series of different tasks leading to a specific goal. In this case it is the goal that is the point, rather than the actions. Examples are organising a new marketing campaign, writing a book proposal, submitting plans for a new extension, approving new contractors and so on.

Because they are not repetitive in nature they are best dealt with by being split down into smaller tasks.

These tasks can then be brought forward for action by being put into the task diary. A small number of tasks can be put down for tomorrow's date. Larger or more complicated projects can be spread a few tasks at a time over a week or more.

When scheduling a complex project in the task diary it's useful to put in plenty of items like the following in order to keep the project on track:

- Think about . . .
- Discuss . . . with . . .
- Make decision about . . .
- Plan . . .
- Review . . .

Each of these may generate a series of further tasks, which can be dealt with in their turn by means of the task diary.

You may get some projects that are too short to be classed as continuous projects but don't lend themselves to being broken down into sub-tasks because the actions are essentially repetitive. An example would be 'sort out bookshelves'. The task is too big to complete in one day. The best way to deal with such tasks is to re-enter them each day in the task list until the project is completed.

Prioritising projects – doing the least urgent things first

The order in which you tackle projects makes a profound difference to the way you work. Of course, you should never take on any project unless you have time to do it properly. But it's still important to get them in the right order. We've already seen that the two most common ways of prioritising are by importance and by urgency. It would actually be truer to say that the two most common ways of *talking about* prioritising are by importance and urgency – because in the real world prioritising by urgency is the one that normally comes out on top. We've already seen that the problem with prioritising by importance – should anyone be foolish enough to do it consistently – is that the neglected 'unimportant' stuff would eventually gum up the works.

I don't in fact believe that anyone consistently prioritises by importance because it is virtually impossible to do. Prioritising by urgency is far more common, and many people, consciously or unconsciously, prioritise by urgency on a more or less continuous basis.

Unfortunately, the effect of using urgency as our criterion for what to do first is very detrimental. The tendency is to wait to do something *until* it becomes urgent. The result is that life is lived in a constant rush of impending deadlines. This is very stressful, the quality of work is lowered and reliability is lessened. The benefits of working 'little and often' on a project are seldom realised. Finally, one is never able to take full advantage of the amount of time that one has been allocated to complete a project. It doesn't matter whether you have a week or a month to complete a report. Either way it will be finished in a rush in the last couple of days before the deadline. In fact it is often *more* likely to be finished on time the shorter the time allowed – after a month's worth of procrastination it may be almost impossible to get started on the report.

It actually makes more sense to use as one's guiding principle the concept of prioritising by reverse order of urgency. In other words, do the *least urgent* things first. This sounds crazy at first glance. Let's look at why it works.

When people talk about how urgent something is, they are generally including two completely different things:

1 Things that are urgent because they really are urgent in themselves (e.g. evacuating a building when it's on fire, getting a front-page scoop ready for the next edition).
2 Things that are urgent only because they haven't been done earlier (e.g. getting the report we have been putting off finished by the deadline).

For most people, the second category of urgent things greatly outnumbers the first. What this means is that most of our urgent work is urgent only because we haven't got started on it sooner. Does the principle of tackling the *least urgent* things first make more sense to you now? If we follow it on a consistent basis, nothing will get left undone for so long that it becomes an emergency. *Real* emergencies will need to be responded to quickly, of course, but their disruptive effect will be much less because all the artificially induced emergencies have been removed.

Delegation

No discussion about projects would be complete without saying something about delegation. The subject is a large one and worth a book on its own, so I am only going to look at it from a time-management point of view. Delegation is an area where one's own time management is affected very directly by the quality of other people's time management.

I am using the word 'delegation' to cover all situations where you pass work that is your responsibility to another person, whether or not that person is a subordinate or an employee. In this sense delegation may be sideways or even upwards.

Particularly when delegating downwards, you want to encourage the other person not only to get the delegated work done but also to use good time-management practices when doing so. The greatest sin you can commit when you delegate is to sit on work for days or weeks and then produce it at the last minute as an emergency. This will destroy your subordinates' ability to plan their work.

You can tell when you have a problem with delegation because you constantly find yourself using the sentence, 'It's quicker to do it yourself'. You should see this as a sign that your delegating skills are not as good as they should be. In other words, it is you who are at fault, not the person you are delegating to.

So here are the top seven ways of increasing your effectiveness at delegating:

Never sit on work – delegate it as soon as possible
There are two main reasons why people sit on work and

delegate it at the last minute. One is that their time-management skills are bad, so they procrastinate over doing anything about that particular piece of work. The other is that their delegation skills are bad, and they hope that they will galvanise the recipient of the work into action if it's presented to them as an emergency. Frequently, of course, both reasons are in play.

Both these reasons are faults in the person who is doing the delegating. Remember, the later you leave it to delegate to someone else, the more disruption you are causing to the rest of his or her work.

Allow a buffer when setting a deadline
Don't give deadlines that leave you with no leeway. Always allow a sufficient buffer to give you time to chase the work if it is late without throwing you into an emergency situation. You need also to make sure that you have left yourself adequate time to process your share of the work when it is returned to you.

Be specific
Always be quite clear about what you want done and by when. Make it clear that you expect the deadline to be met.

Give intermediate deadlines
All but the simplest projects should be given intermediate deadlines. Research has shown that giving intermediate deadlines greatly increases the likelihood of a project being completed on time. It also increases the quality of the finished work.

When giving intermediate deadlines you should be quite specific about what is to be achieved by the deadline.

Don't use vague phrases like 'Come back in a week and we'll have a look at how you're getting on'. Do give clear definite instructions like 'Draw up your detailed plan for Phase 1 and we'll meet at this time next week to discuss it'.

Remind before a deadline

A day or so before an intermediate or final deadline, issue a reminder that you are expecting the work back on the deadline. You can use your task diary to keep track of these reminders. There's quite a skill in picking the right point for reminding someone about a deadline. You want to make it close enough so they have no excuse for forgetting it. You also want to make it far enough in advance so that if they've not yet done anything about the work they have time to do it. One or two days should be fine in most cases. The important thing is to remind them that *you* haven't forgotten about the deadline!

Follow up immediately

If the person misses the deadline, you must follow up immediately. If they don't hear anything from you they will think it doesn't matter. Again, use your task diary to remind you to check that you have received the completed work by the correct date.

Don't listen to excuses

Make it quite clear that you are not interested in *why* a deadline has been missed. You are interested only in *when* the work will be completed. Focus on that point exclusively. Make them give you a new completion date and hold them to it.

Test yourself

How would you deal with the following situations?

1 You want to get fit so you decide to take up exercise cycling.

2 You have been asked to draw up recommendations for reorganising the post room. The managing committee will consider your recommendations at their July meeting. It is January.

3 You have just attended the monthly meeting of the requisitions committee. You agreed to have a quick word with some of the heads of department about their needs and report back to the next meeting of the committee.

4 You are due to go to the next meeting of the harmonisation committee. You get out the minutes of the last meeting and are horrified to see that you agreed to check the progress on Section VI, para. 24, subpara. 6A.iic of the previous minutes with a view to updating the committee. You had forgotten all about it.

5 You are fed up with the fact that invoices keep getting sent out late. You decide you will sort it out when you can find the time.

6 One of your account executives tells you that she hasn't been able to find the time to investigate the standard product-services contract. She was supposed to be briefing you about it today.

7 Congratulations! You have landed a contract with a publisher for your first novel. Delivery of the completed manuscript is due in eight months' time.

8 You realise that your on-line payments system is

showing its age and will need a complete revamp before too long.

Answers

1 This is a continuous project. It needs to be scheduled for a precise time of day. You probably don't want to do it every day – probably three times a week would be fine. Draw up a schedule and stick to it. The more exact you are about keeping to the timings you have drawn up, the more quickly it will become a habit. Don't make the mistake of adding more continuous projects than you can cope with.

2 You have six months for a task that won't take anything like as long – and therein lies the danger. It is easy to put this sort of project off until it becomes urgent. Remember the rule – *do the least urgent things first* – and get on with it straight away. Come July you will be so glad you did!

3 You have·one month to 'have a quick word' with various people. It's very easy to put this off because it doesn't seem urgent. The result is likely to be that you get into a rush at the last minute. Another case for applying the *do the least urgent things first* rule.

4 Don't you wish you had heard of the *do the least urgent things first* rule? As it is, you are going to have to apologise to the committee for your failure to take action. Now that you *have* heard of the rule, make use of it in future!

5 What do you mean, 'when you can find the time'? You know perfectly well that means never. This is an ideal candidate for the current-initiative spot. I suggest you keep a list of things for that spot and knock them off one by one.

6 Make it quite clear you are not interested in *why* she is late. Remind her of the consequences of her lateness and ask *when* she will be ready to brief you. Make it clear you expect it to happen this time.

7 Eight months sounds a very long time. Don't be deceived – start writing the book now. Remember: *do the least urgent things first!*

8 As a rough guide:

- projects with deadlines should be dealt with under the *least urgent things first* rule.
- Projects without any deadline should be considered as candidates for the current initiative slot.

As this project has only a vague time indication – 'before too long' – it is best dealt with as a current initiative to get it up and running.

15

Sorting Out Systems

The time you spend on systems is seldom wasted, and usually repays itself thousands of times over.

We have already discussed how the systems that we use, or fail to use, can support or devastate our work. The most important system of course is one's system for processing work – which is what we have been discussing in the whole of the rest of this book. In this chapter I want to take a brief look at some other common systems that are used to support us in our working environments.

Whenever things go wrong in your work it's always worth looking at the system you are using. Here's a typical system for handling email, which is used by thousands of people: 'When a new email comes in I break off from what I am doing to check what it is. I will either deal with it immediately or leave it for later.'

Here's another person describing their system: 'I check incoming email at intervals throughout the day to see if anything requires an instant reply. Otherwise I leave it all until the following day, when I clear it all in one batch.'

What are going to be the results of using these two systems? Notice how little the difference is between them. In both cases incoming email is checked and some of it is actioned and some of it is left. The main difference is in how closely defined the actions are. In the first there is no definition of which emails will get actioned immediately and which won't. There is also no defined time that the remainder will be dealt with. In the second, it is closely defined when each email will be actioned.

If you examine the likely results of the two systems you will see that the first will result in constant interruptions and is also liable to build up a backlog. The second will result in far fewer interruptions and will clear all the email within a day. The second is also likely to be far faster, as most emails will be dealt with together rather than haphazardly.

These two systems for dealing with email are not that different in how they look, but the difference in results is considerable. This is just one example of how very small changes to the way we do things can make a huge difference. Another example would be the difference between coming back from a meeting and throwing your briefcase into a corner and coming back from a meeting and emptying the contents of your briefcase into your in-tray. In the first you are ensuring that your briefcase becomes a mobile dump of unactioned papers. In the second you are ensuring that the papers in your briefcase get actioned quickly and efficiently.

Good systems are not just a matter of personal convenience or efficiency. Systems can make or break a business. Many businesses have gone bust because of the deficiencies of their invoicing systems or their credit-control systems. Even more do far less well than they could be doing because they don't have good systems for customer follow-up.

However, my purpose here is not to teach you how to set up good business systems, but to look at some of the systems that may be able to support you in your personal day-to-day work. I will be looking particularly at the circumstances of people who are working from home and people who do a lot of travelling. But much of what I will be saying may well still apply to you even if these aren't your exact circumstances. In all cases the need is to provide a structure that will support you in what you wish to do. It's a good rule to remember that if you can get the structure right, your actions will generally be right too.

Working from home

If we look at the peculiar circumstances of people who work from home, the first thing we note is that they tend to lack a supporting structure. They don't have the sort of structure that comes just from being in an office surrounded by colleagues and co-workers.

If you work in a big office, you are going to be surrounded by other workers and you will have a boss controlling your work to a greater or lesser degree. You will have an established pattern of work that helps to keep you in line. You will tend to start work at the same time each day; you will tend to be isolated from domestic issues; you will have more or less clear goals and objects; and you will have people imposing and enforcing deadlines on you.

On top of those things, your office will have a whole range of specialists responsible for such things as pay, accounts, marketing, human resources, pensions, insurance, health and safety, legal, design, etc. You are free to get on with your own work, knowing that other people are responsible for all the other areas.

If you own your own small business and work at home you have none of this. Everything is your responsibility.

You have no one enforcing any boundaries on you. You have no one to task you or hold you to deadlines. You have no supporting departments. Everything has to come from you.

I don't want to make it sound all doom and gloom, because there are huge advantages to working at home. I have worked at home myself by choice for the last twenty years. But it does require thought and organisation to get a good structure going.

The first area to look at is your working hours. If you are having trouble distinguishing between your work and your home life, then it is helpful to make a clear distinction in your mind about when you are working and when you are not. Give yourself as clear working hours as you would have if you were working in an office. A good rule to have is: *when you are working you do nothing but work; when you are not working you do anything but work!*

It doesn't matter what your working hours are as long as you have defined them. One of the benefits of working from home is that you can decide for yourself what your working hours are. If you choose to work from 2 a.m. to 10 a.m. and then take the whole of the rest of the day off that's fine – no one is going to stop you (not if you live on your own, anyway!). The important thing is that you are clear in your own mind about when you are working and when you are not.

Once you've defined your hours you need to make it clear to the other people in your life that these times must be protected. One of the problems with working at home is that other people may expect you to deal with domestic affairs during these times. You need to put boundaries firmly in place here and enforce them.

The best way to look at this subject is to take a step back and imagine that you have a boss – and it's you! As your boss, you tell yourself what your conditions of work are, what time you start and stop work, when your breaks are, whether you are allowed to make personal calls in working hours, what your holiday allowance is, and so on and so forth. As your boss, you also define what your work consists of and task yourself with assignments and deadlines. And, like a boss, you need to be strict in keeping yourself in line.

Filing

One system that makes all the difference in the world to a home-office worker is how they file paper and documents. A good filing system is one where:

- You can quickly lay your hands on the things that you need all the time;
- You can easily find things that you don't need all the time;
- You know exactly where to put stuff without having to think about it.

Most filing systems do not measure up to this. Frequently they are so unwieldy that it's too difficult to find the stuff you need to hand all the time. So you tend to put things like that where you can get at them quickly, i.e. anywhere but in your filing system. Many filing systems are so non-intuitive that you can't find anything that you haven't looked at recently. The result is that you frequently have to waste time searching for things. Many filing systems require quite a lot of mental and physical effort to file things, so unfiled stuff tends to pile up because it's just too much effort to file them properly.

The result of these defects is that many people end up having two filing systems. They have their 'official' one, which is where they are supposed to file things, but don't because it's too much effort. And they have an 'unofficial' one, which consists of various piles of paper and folders, arranged in no sort of order at all.

This is another example of a system that is not very likely to lead to good results. Having a malfunctioning filing system like this can be a real drag on your productivity. Look in the boxes for some advice on how to set up a better system!

Finding stuff quickly

Here's a little trick that may help you to find more quickly the files that you use all the time. If you have your files arranged by subject or in alpha-betical order, you probably find that you have to think quite hard in order to find them. I used to find that quite difficult. First of all I had to remember what the file was called, and then find the right place where it should be. I often found it wasn't where it ought to be but had moved some-how into the wrong place. It was just as difficult when I was putting the file away – I had to think in order to know what to do with it.

By contrast, have you ever noticed how easy it is to find a website address in your browser when the items are ordered so the last used is at the top? It is by far the fastest way of finding something that you use regularly. Our minds are pretty good at remembering how long ago it was when we last used something.

It's very easy to do the same thing with files. Personally, rather than use a filing cabinet, I have all my papers filed in lever arch files arranged on a bookshelf. Whenever I use a file I always put it back at the left end of the top shelf. I move the other files along to give it space. So all the files are now arranged in the order I last used them. Result: I can lay my hands instantly on every file that I use frequently. Another advantage is that I don't have to think about where to put a file when I have finished with it. It always goes in the same spot – the left end of the top shelf.

I found the system worked so well for files that I now use it for books too. No longer do I lose books that I am reading. I know exactly where to put them so that I can find them again. I can also see exactly when I last looked at any particular book. It's a very simple system, but it works!

File for success!

One of the biggest reasons our offices tend to get into chaos is that we simply don't know what to do with half the stuff that comes into our lives. If we don't know what to do with it, we tend to put it down somewhere to deal with 'later'. The inevitable result is piles of unsorted paper and a backlog of work.

One of the most important ways of ensuring that we know what to do with things is to have a filing system that is both easy to operate and completely up to date. Unfortunately, most people, particularly in small businesses, try to work with filing systems that don't properly support them. Remember: we will always tend to follow the path of least resistance. If our filing system is difficult and cumbersome to use then we will tend to avoid using it, which will then make it out of date as well – thus increasing the problem further. On the other hand, if our filing system is fast, instinctive and up to date, it becomes easier to use it than not to use it. The good news is that you can have a fast, instinctive and up-to-date filing system fully operational by tomorrow. Here's how.

The first step is to go out and buy plenty of lever arch files and clear enough space for them on a bookshelf. Forget about folders, ring binders, suspension files and all the rest. Lever arch files on a bookshelf are the best way of filing. They stand upright, don't fall over, can be moved around easily and it's simple to insert and remove papers from them. What's more, you can use dividers to subdivide the contents. You can put things you don't want to punch holes in into a transparent plastic envelope and file the plastic envelope. For very small items such as till receipts I staple them to a larger sheet of paper and file the sheet of paper.

How do you get a totally up-to-date filing system right now? It's easy. Declare your old filing system dead and start completely afresh, opening new files as you need them. Every time you get a new piece of paper, open a new file for it or put it into one of the new files you have already opened. Work the files in the way I suggested in the previous box by putting the files as you use them at the top left-hand end of the bookcase. With lever arch files it's easy to move the files along to accommodate this. Doing it this way you will have a completely fresh and relevant filing system, where you can always lay your hands on the papers you use most often.

Accounts

As a person running one's own business from home it's easiest to do jobs like making entries in the accounts on a daily basis. That means that a very small daily effort keeps you completely on top of the financial state of your business, and VAT and tax returns can be actioned with minimum disruption.

Whatever size business you work in you need to be able to access up-to-date financial information immediately. If your system is not capable of producing it then the system must be redesigned until it does. You cannot exercise any sort of financial control if you are relying on quarterly or (even worse) annual accounts produced weeks or months after the period ends.

Address books

Good contacts are essential for the small business, and too many home businesses don't keep their address books and contact details in good shape. The rule is that every time you contact someone you make sure that the person's entry is correct.

If your address book is way out of date, then remember that this is a kind of backlog. Deal with it by the backlog-clearing procedure. Get the system for making new entries right first, and only then worry about bringing the old information up to date. Even if you never get round to updating the old information, you will find that in a surprisingly short time you have an address book that contains nearly all the contact information that you need to use.

Travelling

Some people's work involves much travelling, and some people have more than one geographical location for their work. If either of these applies to you, then you need to be quite clear in your mind what work you do where. What tends to happen is that work is scooped up indiscriminately to be taken with you. This results in a lack of clear boundaries between your various workplaces and a lack of clarity about what you are trying to achieve. It's much better to define a careful list of what you intend to do and take only the necessary papers. That's much better than bunging everything you can think of into a bag and hoping that you'll catch up somehow.

This has been only a brief look at how investing a little thought in setting up the right systems can make a huge difference to the way that you work. The time you spend on systems is seldom wasted, and usually repays itself thousands of times over.

Test yourself

Which of the following are examples of malfunctioning work systems?

1 You work from home. Your partner keeps interrupting you to ask you to do things around the house or with the children.

2 You keep a supply of stationery items that you need for your work in the top drawer of your desk, where they are to hand.

3 You find it difficult to get your clients to pay up quickly. The bigger the firm, the longer they take to pay and the harder they are to chase.

4 The plants in your offices are all dying from lack of water.

5 You frequently open temporary files to deal with new projects, so you have somewhere to put your drafts, notes, frequently used papers, etc. You usually use an envelope folder, in which you put all the papers. You do not clip them in because you want to be able to get out the individual papers when needed.

6 The milk in the office fridge keeps running out – usually just when you're about to offer a client a cup of coffee.

Answers

1 This is not really a systems malfunction, more an issue of boundaries. However, it needs to be dealt with the same way: by making time to sit down and work out a solution that is acceptable to everyone.

2 This is not a systems malfunction. It's an example of a system that works well.

3 This is not one systems malfunction but two. The first is your system for taking on clients and agreeing terms with them. The second is your system for following up unpaid invoices. The second will be much more effective if you get the first right, but both need attention. This is not a problem that you can afford to neglect – many small firms have gone bust because of this.

4 This is clearly a systems malfunction. It should be clear who is responsibile for this and how and when it is done, and it should be supervised.

5 The problem with opening temporary files like this is that they tend to end up in a heap on a table somewhere. It's much more effective to file your drafts, etc. in a proper project file. Open a new one if necessary. Use the system for filing that I outline in the box and you will be able to find things even more quickly.

6 See Answer 4.

16

Conclusion

Few things are so urgent that they wouldn't be better put off till tomorrow.

The aim of this book was to get you to be 100 per cent creative, ordered and effective. How well has it succeeded in that? Let's try the test again that you took during Chapter 3.

Mark yourself out of ten for creativity _____

Mark yourself out of ten for ordered _____

Now multiply the two scores. That gives you your percentage effectiveness: _____ per cent

If your score isn't as high as you'd like it to be, tick the items that apply to you in the checklist below.

❑ I write out a will-do list for each day.

❑ I aim to complete my will-do list every day.

❑ I write down every additional thing I do which isn't on my list.

❑ If I do not succeed in completing my will-do list more than three days in a row, I carry out an audit of my work to see whether I have too much work, am working inefficiently or am not leaving enough time.

❑ I save up emails and deal with them in one batch the following day.

❑ I save up paper and deal with it in one batch the following day.

- ❏ I save up voicemails and deal with them in one batch the following day.
- ❏ I save up tasks and deal with them in one batch the following day.
- ❏ I have a task diary in which I collect tasks for action the following day or later.
- ❏ The first item on my will-do list every day is my current initiative.
- ❏ I have a list of current initiatives arranged in the order in which I am going to deal with them.

If there are items on the list that you haven't ticked, then these are where you should direct your attention. Good luck!

How to Contact the Author

If you are interested in any of the following:

- becoming one of my coaching clients (limited vacancies available),
- my schedule of classes and seminars,
- subscribing to my free weekly email newsletter,

you can find up-to-date details on my website at www.markforster.net. Alternatively, you can contact me direct at mf@markforster.net

Index